The Transatlantic Economy 2006

Annual Survey of Jobs, Trade and Investment between the United States and Europe

Daniel S. Hamilton and Joseph P. Quinlan

Center for Transatlantic Relations
Johns Hopkins University
Paul H. Nitze School of Advanced International Studies

Hamilton, Daniel S., and Quinlan, Joseph P., *The Transatlantic Economy 2006*. Washington, DC: Center for Transatlantic Relations, 2007.

Center for Transatlantic Relations
American Consortium on EU Studies
EU Center of Excellence Washington, DC
The Paul H. Nitze School of Advanced International Studies
The Johns Hopkins University
1717 Massachusetts Ave., NW, Suite 525
Washington, DC 20036
Tel: (202) 663-5880
Fax (202) 663-5879
Email: transatlantic@jhu.edu
http://transatlantic.sais-jhu.edu
http://american.edu/aces

ISBN 0-9766434-9-9
ISBN-13 978-0-9766434-9-4

Table of Contents

Preface and Acknowledgements

Over the past few years the Center for Transatlantic Relations has offered a series of studies examining the changing nature of the transatlantic economy in a globalizing world.

In earlier works we have examined the deep integration of the U.S. and European economies through both a geographic and sectoral lens in *Deep Integration: How Transatlantic Markets are Leading Globalization* (2005); *Partners in Prosperity: the Changing Geography of the Transatlantic Economy* (2004); and *Drifting Apart or Growing Together: The Continuing Primacy of the Transatlantic Economy* (2003). We have also examined the relationship between investment and national security concerns in *Protecting Our Prosperity: Ensuring Both National Security and the Benefits of Foreign Investment in the United States* (2006).

Each year we also produce an annual survey of the transatlantic economy. This study, **The Transatlantic Economy 2006**, offers the most up to date set of facts and figures describing the deep economic integration binding European nations to America's 50 states.

We would like to thank Andrew Vasylyuk, Laks Ramachandran and Gretchen Demian for their assistance in producing this study.

We are grateful to continuing support for our annual survey from the DaimlerChrysler Corporation Fund as well as generous support from the American Chamber of Commerce to the European Union and its corporate members Boeing, Hill & Knowlton, Houston Consulting Europe, Procter & Gamble, and SAS, which is also a valued corporate sponsor of the Center for Transatlantic Relations.

Daniel S. Hamilton
Joseph P. Quinlan

Executive Summary

- Although recent years have been among the worst of times for transatlantic political relations, they have been the best of times for the transatlantic economy.

- Since hitting a cyclical bottom in 2001/02 due to the bursting of the U.S. technology bubble and the subsequent U.S. recession, transatlantic trade, investment and corporate profits have soared in recent years, with the United States and Europe each leveraging off each other's strengths.

- Despite all the transatlantic political bickering, the hype associated with the rise of China and India, and constant warnings of a transatlantic divorce, the bilateral economic bonds of the United States and Europe have only grown stronger since the beginning of this decade.

- We estimate that the transatlantic economy generates roughly $3.75 trillion in total commercial sales a year and employs up to 14 million workers in mutually 'insourced' jobs on both sides of the Atlantic who enjoy high wages, high labor and environmental standards, and open, largely nondiscriminatory access to each others' markets.

- The transatlantic economy remains at the forefront of globalization: trade and investment ties between the United States and Europe are deeper and thicker than between any other two continents. This is evident from the most recent data available:

Investment First, Trade Second

- The years since the end of the Cold War—the years when the fading "glue" of the Cold War partnership supposedly loosened transatlantic ties— have marked in fact one of the most intense periods of transatlantic integration ever.

- Despite the hype about the significance of NAFTA and the stunning economic rise of Asia, transatlantic investment flows remain quite strong. Over the first half of this decade, for instance, Europe accounted for just over 57% of total U.S. foreign direct investment (FDI) outflows. In turn, Europe accounted for over 75% of total U.S. FDI inflows over the same period.

- In 2005, European investment inflows to the U.S. totaled $66.1 billion, an increase of more than $13 billion over 2004 levels. Europe accounted for roughly two-thirds of total global investment flows into the United States in 2005, slightly less as a percentage of the overall total than in 2004, but still far and away the most significant source of foreign investment in the U.S. economy.

- European FDI to the U.S. remained strong in the first half of 2006, with inflows of $61 billion -- roughly 3 times the level of the same period for 2005.

- 2005 was an unusual year for U.S. investment flows to the world, including to Europe, due to the passage of the American Jobs Creation Act of 2004. This act offered a one-time incentive to U.S. multinationals to repatriate earnings back to the United States. For a variety of reasons, many American firms did just that. Rather than reinvesting their earnings in European operations, as is often the case, many U.S. firms repatriated capital back home. Because reinvested earnings are one of three key components of foreign direct investment, a decline in reinvested earnings is typically associated with a decline in total FDI. Indeed, in 2005 there was a net outflow of U.S. FDI from Europe of $37.5 billion, in contrast to a net inflow of $93 billion in 2004. As discussed, 2005 was an atypical year due to this one-off legislative provision of tax incentives.

- In 2006 strong U.S. FDI flows to Europe quickly resumed their normal pattern, totaling $51 billion in the first half of the year alone, up 53% from the same period in 2005. Europe accounted for 47% of total US FDI in the first half of 2006.

- Even with the 2005 anomaly, U.S. investment flows to Europe considerably outweighed U.S. investment elsewhere. For example, while U.S. foreign direct investment to China has increased sharply over the past few years, total U.S. investment in China last year ($1.6 billion) was just 23% of total U.S. investment in Belgium in 2005. U.S. investment in Germany was roughly four-and-a-half times larger than U.S. investment in China in 2005.

- U.S. investment in France, while down due to the repatriation of U.S. reinvested earnings in 2005, was still some 16.7% greater than what U.S. firms invested in India.

- On a historic cost basis, the U.S. investment position in Europe was nearly three times larger than corporate America's investment position in all of Asia at the end of 2005.

- U.S. investment stakes in Italy at the end of 2005, some $26 billion on a historic cost basis, were greater than the combined U.S. investment position in China and India ($25.4 billion).

- Throughout this decade Europe has retained its position as the primary target of U.S. investment around the world. Between 2000 and 2005, U.S. companies invested more than four times as much in the UK than in China/Hong Kong. U.S. investments in China are accelerating, but from a low base. Over the course of this decade, U.S. investments in China/Hong Kong have been slightly less than U.S. investments in Ireland.

- While U.S. affiliates on the whole target local European markets, many are increasingly leveraging some European nations as export platforms. U.S. affiliate sales in Ireland, Belgium, the Netherlands, Switzerland and Hungary are greater in third markets and the U.S. than in the local market. The same trend is visible in Finland and Sweden.

- European affiliates of U.S. companies are also major employers in many European nations. Affiliates directly employ more than 1 million workers in the UK; 601,700 in Germany; 562,800 in France; 238,500 in Italy; 197,200 in Spain; 120,000 in Belgium. The U.S. affiliate work force in Poland has grown from a modest level a decade ago to 90,700 – among the largest in all of Europe. These figures tend to understate total employment levels, because they do not include indirect employment or jobs supported by transatlantic trade, which are also substantial.

Europe as a Key Source of Capital for the U.S.

- Europe is not only a critical source of revenue for U.S. multinationals, it is also a key supplier of capital or liquidity for the debt-stretched United States. In 2005, European purchases of U.S. assets (U.S. treasuries, government agency bonds, corporate bonds and U.S. equities) soared to a record $470.4 billion. The bulk of the capital came from the United Kingdom ($362 billion), Europe's primary financial hub and capital transit point for investment from the Middle East, Russia and other points. However, even after excluding inflows from the UK, EU capital inflows to the U.S. totaled $108 billion in 2005, a 76% jump from 2004.

The Transatlantic Boom in Profits

- Europe is the most important commercial market in the world for corporate America by a wide yet unappreciated margin. In 2005, for instance, U.S. foreign affiliate income from Europe surged to a record $106 billion, a figure equivalent to just over 46% of total U.S. foreign affiliate income.

- U.S. foreign affiliate earnings of $106 billion in Europe in 2005 were more than double affiliate earnings derived from all of Asia ($50.4 billion).

- In 2005 U.S. affiliates posted record earnings in the United Kingdom ($19.9 billon), Ireland ($12.4 billion), Germany ($6.7 billion), Italy ($2.9 billion), and Norway ($2.7 billion).

- Total U.S. foreign affiliate income earned in Poland, Hungary and the Czech Republic has soared over this decade, even if from a small base. U.S. affiliate income in these three countries collectively totaled $1.5 billion in 2005, triple the level of 2000. U.S. affiliates earned more in these three markets last year than they did in India ($1.1 billion).

- Just as Europe is the most important foreign market in the world for American firms, the U.S. is the top overseas market for European multinationals. Indeed, strong sales and profits in the United States has been a catalyst behind Europe's booming equity markets of the past few years.

- In fact, to an important degree Corporate Europe's earnings boom has been "Made in America," with annual earnings of European affiliates in the U.S. soaring to a record high in 2005. Between 2001 and 2005 European affiliate earnings in the U.S. rose more than five-fold, from a cyclical low of $14 billion in 2001 to $77 billion in 2005. Last year, the combination of strong U.S. economic growth and a weak euro versus the dollar helped boost affiliate income of European affiliates to record highs.

- French affiliate earnings in the U.S. surged 30% in 2005 from the prior year, to a record $11.4 billion. Income earned by German affiliates in the U.S. rose by nearly 26% in 2005, to a record $7.8 billion. British affiliates posted usually strong earnings, with affiliate income rising to nearly $30 billion in 2005, a 50% jump from the prior year.

Transatlantic Service Ties Have Only Grown Stronger -- Driven by Investment

- The service economies of the United States and Europe have never been as intertwined as they are today, notably in such activities as financial services, telecommunications, utilities, insurance, advertising, computer services, and other related activities.

- Foreign affiliate sales of services on both sides of the Atlantic have exploded over the past decade. In fact, affiliate sales of services have not only supplemented trade in services to become a viable second channel of delivery for U.S. and European multinationals, they have become the overwhelming mode of delivery in a rather short period of time.

- Sales of services of U.S. foreign affiliates in Europe soared again in 2005, rising to a record $265 billion. U.S. affiliate sales of services were 81% larger than U.S. service exports to Europe last year. The United Kingdom accounted for nearly 40% of U.S. foreign affiliate sales of services in 2005. On a global basis, Europe accounted for 53% of total U.S. affiliate sales of services last year.

- Sales of services by U.S. affiliates of European firms have also soared over the past decade. As Europe's investment position in services has expanded in the U.S., so have Europe's foreign affiliate sales of services. In 2005, affiliate sales of services in the U.S. totaled $260.6 billion, more than double U.S. service imports from Europe in the same year ($123 billion). In total, Europe accounted for 68% of total U.S. affiliate sales last year.

- Transatlantic trade in services also remains substantial. Europe accounted for 40% of total U.S. service exports and for 44% of total U.S. service imports in 2005. Five of the top ten U.S. export markets for services in 2005 were in Europe. The United Kingdom ranked first, Germany fifth, France sixth, Switzerland eighth and the Netherlands tenth. Similarly, among the top ten importers of services to the U.S., five were from Europe in 2005. The U.K. ranked first, Germany fourth, France seventh, Switzerland eighth, and the Netherlands ninth.

- The U.S. enjoyed a $22.4 billion trade surplus in services with Europe in 2005; however, that stands in sharp contrast to the U.S. $124 billon trade deficit in goods with Europe in the same year.

Europe's Investment Base in the U.S. Continues to Expand

- On a historic cost basis, Europe's investment stakes in the United States topped $1.1 trillion in 2005, more than triple the level of 1995. No other region of the world has made such a large capital commitment to the U.S than Europe, with the latter accounting for nearly 70% of total U.S. inward investment stock in 2005.

- Corporate Europe's asset base in the U.S. totaled $4.2 trillion in 2004, a rise of 7.7% from the prior year. Europe accounted for over 75% of total foreign-owned assets in the U.S. in 2004.

- European foreign affiliates directly employed over 3.5 million Americans in 2004, with British firms the top employer of U.S. workers. Germany and the Netherlands ranked second and third, respectively.

- The output of European foreign affiliates in the U.S. rose to $337 billion in 2004, a 7.5% increase from the prior year. European firms accounted for 65% of total foreign affiliate output in the U.S. in 2004.

European-U.S. State Linkages

- The Southeastern United States ranked as the top investment region for British, French, Dutch and Swedish firms in 2004. German firms invested the most in the Great Lakes region, while the Mideast was the region of most Italian and Swiss investment in 2004.

- In 2004, Texas ranked as the top U.S. state for European investment as a whole and a leading target for French investment in particular. Europe's investment stake in Texas topped $55.3 billion in 2004, a slight decrease from $57.5 billion in 2003. European affiliates directly employed 228,000 workers in Texas in 2004 (similar employment figure in 2003).

- In 2004, California attracted $45.1 billion in European investment, a slight decrease from $45.8 billion in 2003. European affiliates directly employed 337,400 California workers with roughly one-quarter of these jobs in manufacturing activities, a decrease in jobs from 363,300 in 2003. California was a top investment target for British, Swiss, and Dutch firms. In 2004, European affiliates created 67,300 manufacturing jobs in California, higher than in any other state.

- In 2004, New York ranked as the third largest U.S. state for European investment, attracting $39.1 billion in 2004, slight decrease from $41.1 billion in 2003. European affiliates directly employed 289,400 workers in New York in 2004, a decrease from 293,600 in 2003. New York was top investment site for French investment, and substantial investments by German and Swiss financial pharmaceutical firms were clustered around New York and New Jersey.

- European affiliates account for over 50,000 manufacturing jobs in each of five different states -- California, Texas, Pennsylvania, North Carolina, and Ohio.

Chapter 1
The Transatlantic Economy Today: Jobs, Trade, and Investment

The transatlantic partnership has traveled a rocky road over the past few years. The bursting of the U.S. technology bubble in 2001, and the subsequent U.S. recession, triggered a sharp decline in transatlantic trade, investment and profits early in the decade.

Next came the terrorist attacks on the United States on September 11, 2001. At first, 9/11 rendered transatlantic bonds even stronger as Europeans rallied around a wounded United States. However, the post-9/11 moment of transatlantic solidarity proved to be quite fleeting, and quickly gave way to transatlantic bitterness and acrimony over the war in Iraq. Diplomatic relations between the U.S. and many European countries hit new lows in 2003 and 2004.

In addition to the U.S.-led war in Iraq, other forces have weighed on the transatlantic partnership over the past few years, including the passage of the Sarbanes-Oxley Act in mid-2002, which has tempered, to a degree, transatlantic mergers and acquisition in particular and cross-border capital flows in general. China's economic rise and Iran's nuclear program have also added more stress and strain to the transatlantic partnership, with the U.S. and Europe responding to each challenge differently and in some cases, at cross purposes.

The Doha round of multilateral trade negotiations, the Kyoto climate treaty, sector-specific trade spats, disputes over access to airline passenger data, human rights concerns at Guantanamo Bay and Abu Ghraib, instability in the Middle East—all of these issues have chipped away at the transatlantic partnership as well, testing the bonds that have made U.S.-EU collaboration a hallmark of the global economy for the past half century.

Yet despite all of the above, and notwithstanding the last few years being among the worst of times for the transatlantic partnership, it has also been among the best of times for the transatlantic economy.

Since hitting a cyclical bottom in 2001/02, transatlantic trade, investment and corporate profits have soared, with both the United States and Europe leveraging off each other's strengths. Strong economic growth in the United States has been a key catalyst in boosting corporate earnings in Europe, which in turn has helped promote more investment and employment growth across the region. Meanwhile, the enlargement of the European Union, coupled with micro reform in various key nations, such as Germany, has been a windfall for U.S. multinationals, many which have enjoyed record profits growth over the past three years.

2005 Another Record Setting Year for the Transatlantic Economy

The following all time highs were recorded in 2005:

Transatlantic Income	
U.S. Foreign Affiliate Income from Europe	$ 106 billion
U.S. Foreign Affiliate Income from Austria	$ 1.6 billion
U.S. Foreign Affiliate Income from Czech Republic	$ 439 million
U.S. Foreign Affiliate Income from Denmark	$ 1 billion
U.S. Foreign Affiliate Income from Finland	$ 622 million
U.S. Foreign Affiliate Income from Germany	$ 6.7 billion
U.S. Foreign Affiliate Income from Ireland	$ 12.4 billion
U.S. Foreign Affiliate Income from Italy	$ 2.9 billion
U.S. Foreign Affiliate Income from Netherlands	$ 20.4 billion
U.S. Foreign Affiliate Income from Norway	$ 2.7 billion
U.S. Foreign Affiliate Income from Portugal	$ 430 million
U.S. Foreign Affiliate Income from U.K.	$ 19.9 billion
Foreign Affiliate Income from the U.S.: Europe	$ 77 billion
Foreign Affiliate Income from the U.S.: Denmark	$ 507 million
Foreign Affiliate Income from the U.S.: France	$ 11.4 billion
Foreign Affiliate Income from the U.S.: Germany	$ 7.8 billion
Foreign Affiliate Income from the U.S.: Ireland	$ 1.4 billion
Foreign Affiliate Income from the U.S.: Italy	$ 700 million
Foreign Affiliate Income from the U.S.: Netherlands	$ 16.8 billion
Foreign Affiliate Income from the U.S.: Norway	$ 243 million
Foreign Affiliate Income from the U.S.: Spain	$ 339 million
Foreign Affiliate Income from the U.S.: U.K.	$ 29.8 billion

Investment	
U.S. Foreign Direct Investment to France	$ 7.0 billion
U.S. Foreign Direct Investment to Czech Republic	$ 700 million
U.S. Foreign Direct Investment to Finland	$ 545 million
U.S. Foreign Direct Investment to Russia	$ 1.6 billion
U.S. Foreign Direct Investment from Norway	$ 2.9 billion
U.S. Foreign Direct Investment from Spain	$ 1.7 billion
European Net Purchases of U.S. Securities	$ 496.1 billion
European Net Purchases of U.S. Treasuries	$ 167.0 billion
European Net Purchases of U.S. Corporate Bonds	$ 225.6 billion
French Net Purchases of U.S. Securities	$ 30.9 billion
French Net Purchases of U.S. Treasuries	$ 9.6 billion
French Net Purchases of U.S. Corporate Bonds	$ 13.2 billion
French Net Purchases of U.S. Equities	$ 7.7 billion
U.K. Net Purchases of U.S. Securities	$ 362 billion
U.K. Net Purchases of U.S. Treasuries	$ 134.1 billion
U.K. Net Purchases of U.S. Corporate Bonds	$ 169 billion
U.S. Net Purchases of French Securities	$ 11.2 billion
U.S. Net Purchases of Spanish Securities	$ 5.8 billion
U.S. Net Purchases of Swedish Securities	$ 10.7 billion

Source: Bureau of Economic Analysis; U.S. Department of Treasury

Ironically, despite all the cross-border bickering, the hype associated with the rise of China and India, and constant warnings of a transatlantic divorce, the bilateral economic bonds between the United States and Europe have only grown stronger since the beginning of this decade. The transatlantic economy remains at the forefront of globalization, with trade and investment ties deeper and thicker between the United States and Europe than between any other two continents. This is evident from this survey, which paints a picture of continuing prosperity for both parties.

We estimate that the transatlantic economy continues to generate close to $3.75 trillion in total commercial sales a year and employs up to 14 million workers in mutually "insourced" jobs on both sides of the Atlantic. These workers enjoy high wages and high labor and environmental standards.

Despite the hype about the significance of NAFTA and the stunning economic rise of Asia, transatlantic investment flows remain quite strong. Over the first half of this decade, for instance, Europe accounted for just over 57% of total U.S. foreign direct investment (FDI) outflows. In turn, Europe accounted for over 75% of total U.S. FDI inflows over the same period. In 2005, European investment inflows to the U.S. totaled $66.1 billion, an increase of more than $13 billion over 2004 levels. Europe accounted for roughly two-thirds of total global investment flows into the United States in 2005, slightly less as a percentage of the overall total than in 2004, but still far and away the most significant source of foreign investment in the U.S. economy. European FDI to the U.S. remained strong in the first half of 2006, with inflows of $61 billion—roughly three times the level of the same period for 2005.

2005 was an unusual year for U.S. investment flows to the world, including to Europe, due to the passage of the American Jobs Creation Act of 2004. This act offered a one-time incentive to U.S. multinationals to repatriate earnings back to the United States. For a variety of reasons, many American firms did just that. Rather than reinvesting their earnings in European operations, as is often the case, many U.S. firms repatriated capital back home. Because reinvested earnings are one of three key components of foreign direct investment, a decline in reinvested earnings is typically associated with a decline in total FDI. Indeed, in 2005 there was a net outflow of U.S. FDI from Europe of $37.5 billion, in contrast to a net inflow of $93 billion in 2004. As discussed, 2005 was an atypical year due to this one-off legislative provision of tax incentives.

In 2006, however, strong U.S. FDI flows to Europe quickly resumed their normal pattern, totaling $51 billion in the first half of the year alone, up 53% from the same period in 2005. Europe accounted for 47% of total US FDI in the first half of 2006.

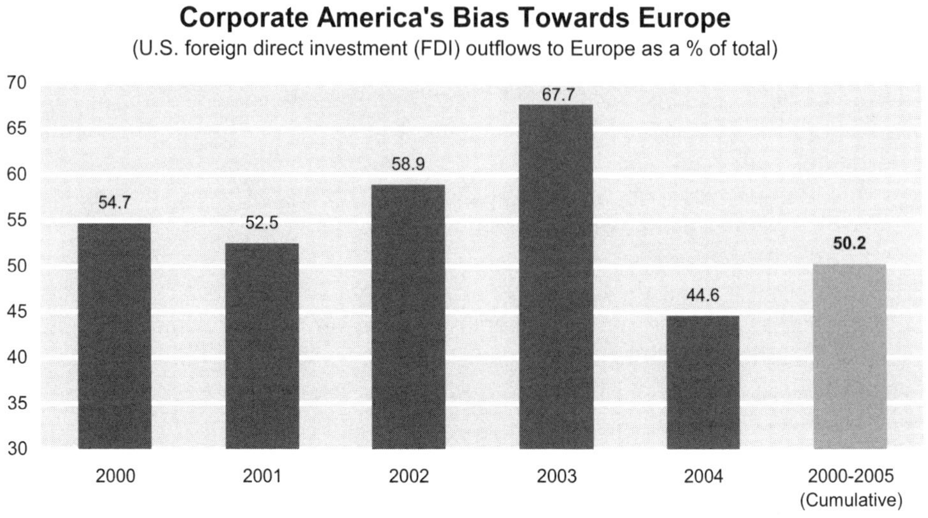

Source: Bureau of Economic Analysis

Even with the 2005 anomaly, U.S. investment flows to Europe considerably outweighed U.S. investment elsewhere. For example, while U.S. foreign direct investment to China has increased sharply over the past few years, total U.S. investment in China in 2005 ($1.6 billion) was just 23% of total U.S. investment in Belgium in that same year. U.S. investment in Germany was roughly four-and-a-half times larger than U.S. investment in China in 2005. U.S. investment in France, while down due to the repatriation of U.S. reinvested earnings in 2005, was still some 16.7% greater than what U.S. firms invested in India.

On a historic cost basis, the U.S. investment position in Europe was nearly three times larger than corporate America's investment position in all of Asia at the end of 2005. U.S. investment stakes in Italy at the end of 2005, some $26 billion on a historic cost basis, were greater than the combined U.S. investment position in China and India ($25.4 billion).

Europe is not only a critical source of revenue for U.S. multinationals, it is also a key supplier of capital or liquidity for the debt-stretched United States. In 2005, European purchases of U.S. assets (U.S. treasuries, government agency bonds, corporate bonds and U.S. equities) soared to a record $470.4 billion. The bulk of the capital came from the United Kingdom ($362 billion), Europe's primary financial hub and capital transit point for investment from the Middle East, Russia and other points. However, even after excluding inflows from the UK, EU capital inflows to the U.S. totaled $108 billion in 2005, a 76% jump from 2004.

Europe is the most important commercial market in the world for corporate America by a wide yet unappreciated margin. In 2005, for instance, U.S. foreign affiliate income from Europe surged to a record $106 billion, a figure equivalent to just over 46% of total U.S.

foreign affiliate income. U.S. foreign affiliate earnings of $106 billion in Europe in 2005 were more than double affiliate earnings derived from all of Asia ($50.4 billion).In 2005 U.S. affiliates posted record earnings in the United Kingdom ($19.9 billon), Ireland ($12.4 billion), Germany ($6.7 billion), Italy ($2.9 billion), and Norway ($2.7 billion).

Euroland Gross Purchases of U.S. Securities 1988-2005

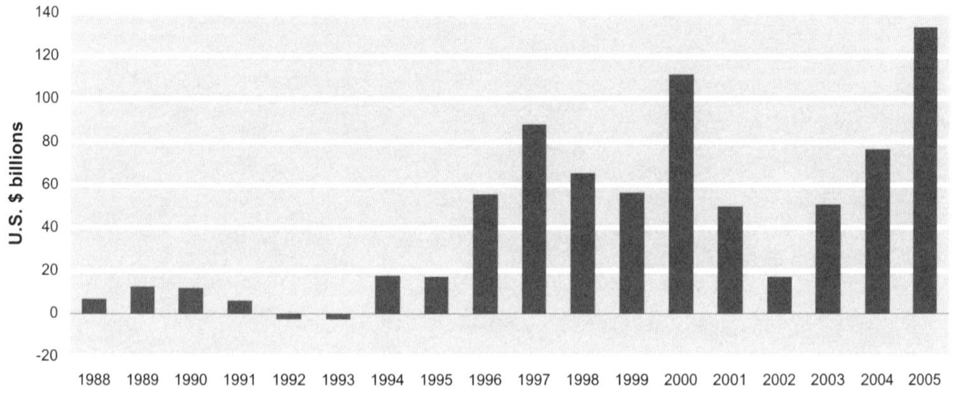

Excludes purchases from the United Kingdom
Source: U.S. Department of the Treasury

Total U.S. foreign affiliate income earned in Poland, Hungary and the Czech Republic has soared over this decade, even if from a small base. U.S. affiliate income in these three countries collectively totaled $1.5 billion in 2005, triple the level of 2000. U.S. affiliates earned more in these three markets last year than they did in India ($1.1 billion), a much larger and over-hyped market.

Just as Europe is the most important foreign market in the world for American firms, the U.S. is the top overseas market for European multinationals. Indeed, strong sales and profits in the United States has been a catalyst behind Europe's booming equity markets of the past few years. In fact, to an important degree Corporate Europe's earnings boom has been "Made in America," with annual earnings of European affiliates in the U.S. soaring to a record high in 2005. Between 2001 and 2005 European affiliate earnings in the U.S. rose more than five-fold, from a cyclical low of $14 billion in 2001 to $77 billion in 2005. In 2005 the combination of strong U.S. economic growth and a weak euro versus the dollar helped boost affiliate income of European affiliates to record highs.

French affiliate earnings in the U.S. surged 30% in 2005 from the prior year, to a record $11.4 billion. Income earned by German affiliates in the U.S. rose by nearly 26% in 2005, to a record $7.8 billion. British affiliates posted usually strong earnings, with affiliate income rising to nearly $30 billion in 2005, a 50% jump from the prior year.

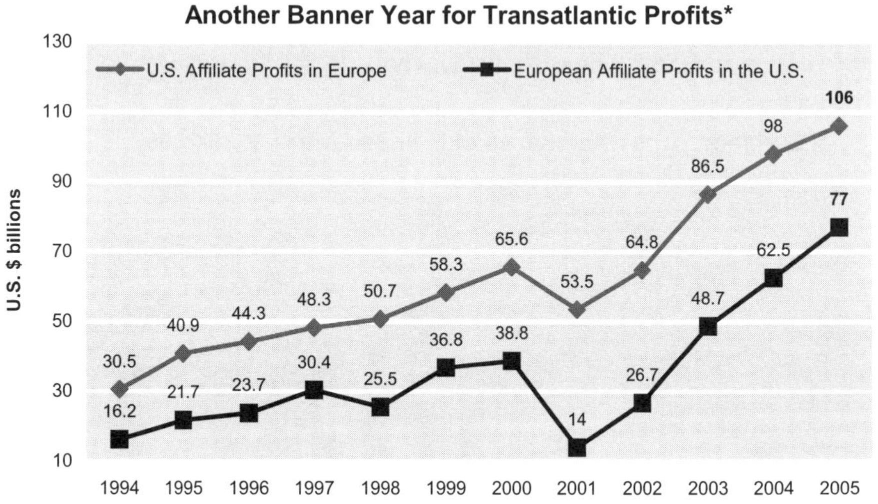

* Income of affiliates
Source: Bureau of Economic Analysis

The service economies of the United States and Europe have never been as intertwined as they are today, notably in such activities as financial services, telecommunications, utilities, insurance, advertising, computer services, and other related activities.

Foreign affiliate sales of services on both sides of the Atlantic have exploded over the past decade. In fact, affiliate sales of services have not only supplemented trade in services to become a viable second channel of delivery for U.S. and European multinationals, they have become the overwhelming mode of delivery in a rather short period of time.

Sales of services of U.S. foreign affiliates in Europe soared again in 2005, rising to a record $265 billion. U.S. affiliate sales of services were 81% larger than U.S. service exports to Europe last year. The United Kingdom accounted for nearly 40% of U.S. foreign affiliate sales of services in 2005. On a global basis, Europe accounted for 53% of total U.S. affiliate sales of services last year.

Sales of services by U.S. affiliates of European firms have also soared over the past decade. As Europe's investment position in services has expanded in the U.S., so have Europe's foreign affiliate sales of services. In 2005, affiliate sales of services in the U.S. totaled $260.6 billion, more than double U.S. service imports from Europe in the same year ($123 billion). In total, Europe accounted for 68% of total U.S. affiliate sales last year.

Transatlantic trade in services also remains substantial. Europe accounted for 40% of total U.S. service exports and for 44% of total U.S. service imports in 2005. Five of the top ten U.S. export markets for services in 2005 were in Europe. The United Kingdom ranked first, Germany fifth, France sixth, Switzerland eighth and the Netherlands tenth. Similarly, among the top ten importers of services to the U.S., five were from Europe in 2005. The U.K. ranked first, Germany fourth, France seventh, Switzerland eighth, and the Netherlands ninth. The U.S. enjoyed a $22.4 billion trade surplus in services with Europe in 2005; however, that stands in sharp contrast to the U.S. $124 billon trade deficit in goods with Europe in the same year.

In sum, the United States and Europe remain each other's most important foreign commercial markets, a fact still not fully appreciated by opinion leaders on both sides of the transatlantic. Put simply, no other commercial artery in the world is as integrated and fused together as the transatlantic economy.

Chapter 2
The Transatlantic Economy Today: Seven Ties that Bind

We have long emphasized the primacy of foreign investment relative to trade in binding the transatlantic economy together. Trade -- the cross-border movement of goods and services -- is a shallow form of integration and emblematic of a nascent, underdeveloped bilateral relationship. In contrast, a commercial relationship resting on the foundation of foreign investment is a deeper form of integration and one in which both parties are extensively embedded and entrenched in each others economies. The transatlantic economy epitomizes the latter.

That said, it has long been our contention that one of the most dangerous deficits affecting the transatlantic partnership is not one of trade, values, or military capabilities but rather a deficit in understanding among opinion leaders of the vital stake Americans and Europeans have developed in the success of each other's respective economies.

Exports and imports have become the most common measurement of cross-border business between nations, but trade alone is a misleading benchmark of international commerce. The real backbone of the transatlantic economy is composed of the unappreciated and little understood activities of U.S.-based affiliates of European parent companies and European-based affiliates of U.S. parent companies.

The Ties that Bind—Quantifying the Transatlantic Economy

Foreign affiliates on both sides of the Atlantic have constructed a formidable commercial infrastructure binding the transatlantic economy together. This infrastructure has been a work in progress for over a century and today represents the deepest and thickest cross-border edifice in the world. However, it remains largely invisible to policy makers on both sides of the ocean.

Over the past few years we have suggested seven key indices that offer a clearer picture of the "deep integration" forces shaping the transatlantic economy. This chapter updates those indices with the latest available data. Overall, each variable grew in size and importance from our last survey.

The Transatlantic World vs. The World Economy

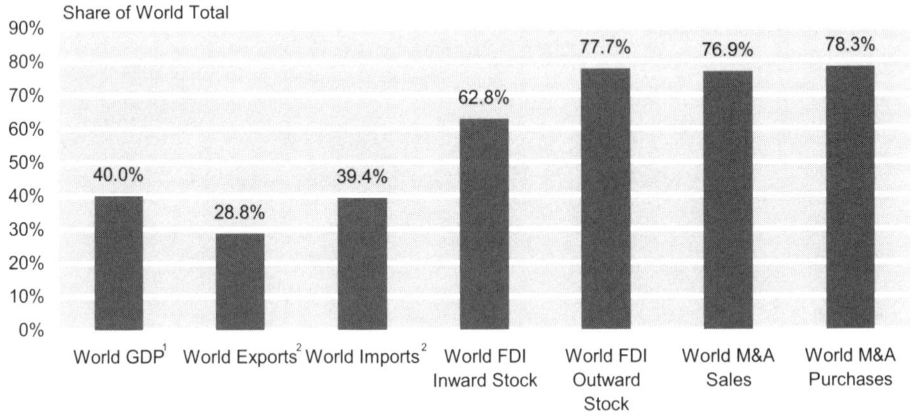

Source: UN, IMF, figures for 2005
(1)Based on PPP estimates, (2) Excluding intra-EU trade

1. Gross Product of Foreign Affiliates

In their own right, U.S. affiliates in Europe and European affiliates in the United States are among the most important economic forces in the world. For instance, the total output of U.S. foreign affiliates in Europe ($460 billion in 2004) and of European affiliates in the U.S. ($336 billion) is greater than the total gross domestic output of most nations. Combined, transatlantic foreign affiliate output (the sum of foreign affiliate output in Europe and the U.S) totaled nearly $800 billion, equivalent to the total output of such nations as South Korea, Brazil and India.

On a global basis, aggregate output of U.S. affiliates topped $824 billion in 2004, with Europe accounting for 56% of the total. The United Kingdom, where U.S. investment ties are deepest, accounted for nearly 30% of total affiliate output in Europe, followed by Germany and France. By sector, output was almost evenly split between services and manufacturing output.

The presence of U.S. affiliates in some European nations is particularly noteworthy. The gross output of American affiliates in Ireland, for instance, represented 14.9% of Ireland's total GDP in 2004, a reflection, in part, of large investment from U.S. technology companies in the "Celtic Tiger." U.S. affiliates accounted for 6.2% of the United Kingdom's aggregate output in the same year, 5.7% of that of Norway, and 5.2% of Belgium's total output. Regarding the latter, it is interesting to note that U.S. foreign affiliate output in Belgium in 2004 ($18.3 billion) was greater than the combined U.S. foreign affiliate output of China and India ($17.2 billion).

In the United States, European affiliates are major economic producers in their own right, with British firms of notable importance. Their U.S. output topped $107 billion in 2004, or one-third of the total. Output from German affiliates operating in the U.S. totaled $66.4 billion, while output from French affiliates was $43 billion in 2004. Overall, foreign affiliates contributed nearly $515 billion to U.S. aggregate production in 2004, with European affiliates accounting for nearly two-thirds of the total.

America's Major Commercial Arteries

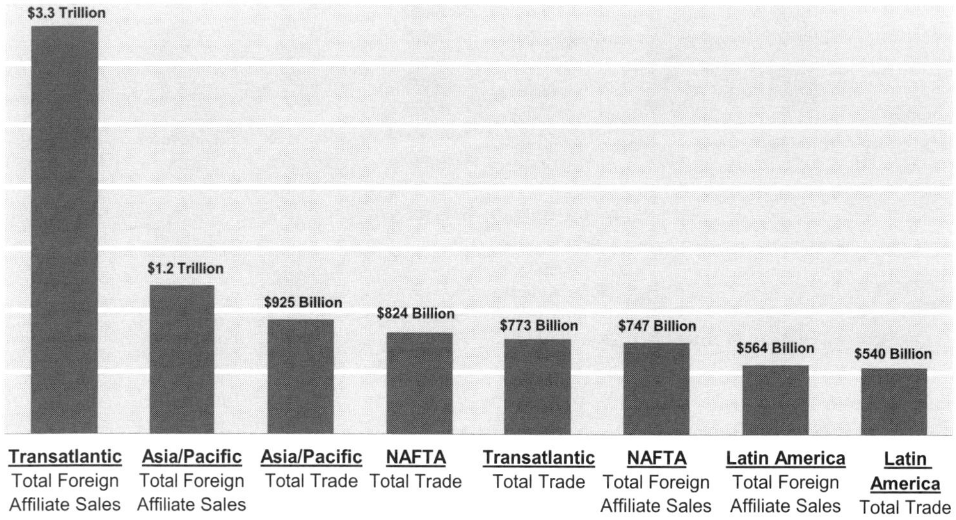

Foreign Affiliate Sales: Data for 2004; Total Trade: Data in goods & services, 2004
Source: U.S. Department of Commerce

2. Assets of Foreign Affiliates

America's global commercial presence has never been larger, with aggregate foreign assets of corporate America totaling $8.8 trillion in 2004. The bulk of these assets—roughly 61%--were located in Europe, with the largest share in the United Kingdom, followed by the Netherlands and Germany. U.S. assets in Germany alone ($419 billion) were greater than total U.S. assets in all of South America. America's corporate assets in the United Kingdom ($1.9 trillion) exceeded total U.S. assets in the entire Asia/Pacific region. Meanwhile, America's asset base in Austria ($29.2 billion) and Portugal ($29 billion) was larger than corporate America's asset base in India ($23.6 billion).

Global Engagement: Foreign Affiliate Sales vs. Trade

$ billions, 2004	U.S. Foreign Affiliate Sales vs. Trade
Global Sales of U.S.-owned Affiliates (G&S)	3768.7
Total U.S. Exports	1151.9
U.S. Sales of Foreign-owned Affiliates[1]	2303.5
U.S. Imports (G&S)	1763.2
European Sales of U.S.-owned Affiliates[1]	1909.7
U.S. Exports to Europe (G&S)	327.7
U.S. Sales of European-owned Affiliates[1]	1391.3
U.S. Imports from Europe (G&S)	444.5

Source: Bureau of Economic Analysis

[1] Majority-owned Affiliates

As for foreign-owned assets in the United States, Europe's stakes are sizable and continue to expand. In 2004, European firms held some $4.2 trillion in U.S. assets, roughly 76% of total foreign assets in the United States. As for the scope of European investment in the U.S., European companies were the top foreign investors in 33 states in 2004, and ranked second in 15 others. Switzerland ranked first as the largest holder of U.S. assets in 2004 ($1.1 trillion), followed closely behind by U.K. firms ($1 trillion).

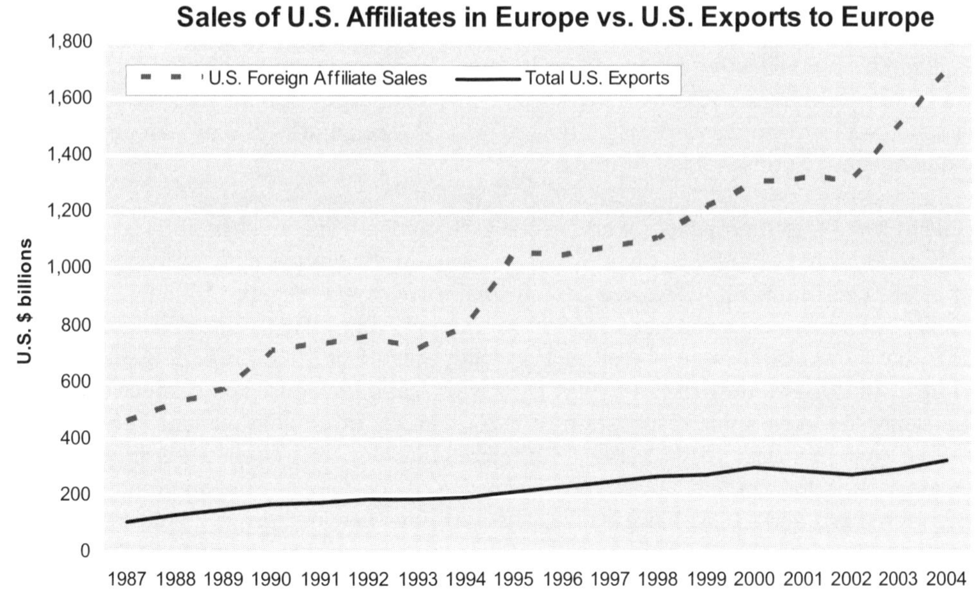

Source: Bureau of Economic Analysis

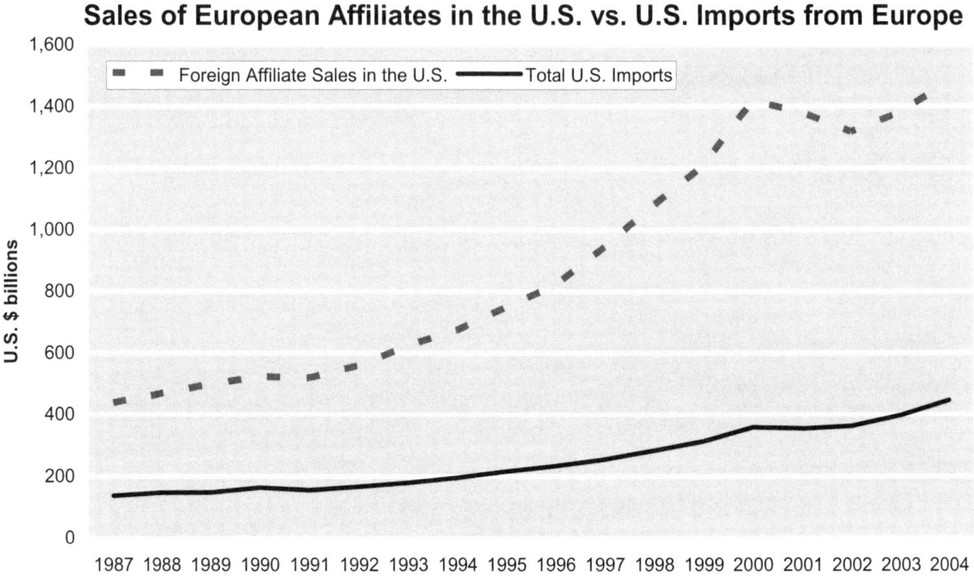

Source: Bureau of Economic Analysis

3. Affiliate Employment

The common perspective is that when it comes to hiring workers overseas, the bulk of corporate America's overseas work forces toils in the developing nations. Reality is different. Most foreign workers on the payrolls of foreign affiliates are employed in the industrialized nations, notably Europe.

Half of the 8.6 million people working for U.S. companies abroad in 2004 were located in Europe. The bulk of these workers were based in the United Kingdom, Germany and France. The European workforce of U.S. majority-owned foreign affiliates was almost evenly split between manufacturing and service workers. That said, it is interesting to note that U.S. affiliates employed just as many manufacturing workers in Europe (1.6 million) in 2004 as they did in 1990. However, while the aggregate number has stayed the same, the geographic distribution of U.S. manufacturing employment in Europe has shifted over the past fifty years. In general, the shift has been towards lower cost locations like Ireland and Spain, at the expense of the United Kingdom and Germany. Between 1990 and 2004, for instance, U.S. affiliate manufacturing employment in the United Kingdom and Germany fell 19.6% and 6.4%, respectively. Meanwhile, manufacturing employment in Ireland soared 37.5% over the same period, while rising 22.4% in Spain. However, even with the decline of manufacturing employment in Germany, the manufacturing workforce of U.S. affiliates in Germany alone totaled 380,000 workers in 2004, more than 47% large than the number of manufactured workers employed in China by U.S. affiliates.

The U.S. - European Employment Balance

Thousands of employees, 2004

Country	European Affiliates of U.S. Companies	U.S. Affiliates of European Companies	Employment Balance
Austria	33.3	9.6	-23.7
Belgium	120.0	130.4	+10.4
Denmark	38.3	60.6	+22.3
Finland	19.6	36.2	+16.6
France	562.8	451.6	-111.2
Germany	601.7	668.6	+66.9
Ireland	82.8	37.4	-45.4
Italy	238.5	102.4	-136.1
Netherlands	175.1	481.1	+306.0
Norway	33.4	9.5	-23.9
Spain	197.2	20.2	-177.0
Sweden	101.2	207.8	+106.6
Switzerland	67.3	383.2	+315.9
United Kingdom	1,166.3	920.8	-245.5
Europe	3,879.3	3,548.0	-331.3

Note: Employment balance "+" favors the United States

Source: Bureau of Economic Analysis

The transportation equipment sector continued to be the largest source of manufactured employment in Europe; wholesale employment was among the largest sources of service-related employment, which includes employment in such areas as logistics, trade, insurance and other service-related activities.

When it comes to affiliate employment, trends in the United States are similar to those in Europe. In other words, despite stories on the European continent about local European companies decamping for cheap labor markets in central Europe or Asia, most foreigners working for European companies outside the EU are American. European majority-owned foreign affiliates directly employed roughly 3.5 million U.S. workers in 2004. The top five employers in the U.S. were firms from the United Kingdom (921,000), Germany (669,000), the Netherlands (481,000), France (452,000), and Switzerland (383,000). European firms employed nearly 70% of the 5.1 million U.S. workers on the payrolls of majority-owned foreign affiliates in 2004.

In the aggregate, the transatlantic workforce directly employed by U.S. and European foreign affiliates in 2004 was nearly 8 million strong. On a global basis, U.S. companies directly employed 10 million workers in 2004, with roughly 43% in Europe. That said, as we have stressed in our last survey, these figures understate the employment effects of mutual investment flows, since these numbers are limited to direct employment, and do not account for indirect employment effects of non-equity arrangements such as strategic alliances, joint ventures and other deals. Moreover, affiliate employment figures do not include jobs supported by transatlantic trade flows. Trade-related employment is substantial in many U.S. states and many European regions.

In total, and adding in indirect employment, we estimate that the transatlantic work force numbers some 12-14 million workers. Europe is by far the most important source of "insourced" jobs in America, and the U.S. is by far the most important source of "insourced" jobs in Europe.

4. Research and Development (R&D) of Foreign Affiliates

While most multinationals still tend to cluster their R&D expenditures and activities in their home country, foreign affiliate R&D has become more prominent over the past decade as firms seek to share development costs, spread risks and tap into the intellectual talent of other nations. Alliances, cross-licensing of intellectual property, mergers and acquisitions and other forms of cooperation have become more prevalent characteristics of the transatlantic economy in the past decade. The internet, in particular, has powered greater transatlantic R&D.

Research and development among U.S. foreign affiliates topped $23 billion in 2003, the last year of available data. The bulk of such activity was carried out in the developed nations, where the largest pool of skilled labor resides. In 2003, U.S. affiliates sunk nearly $15 billion on research and development in Europe, or nearly 65% of total R&D expenditures. The United Kingdom, Germany, France, and Switzerland represented markets where R&D expenditures by U.S. affiliates were greatest.

No comparable country figures for Europe's R&D in the United States is available, although on an aggregate basis, expenditures on R&D performed by majority-owned U.S. affiliates totaled $30 billion in 2004. A significant share emanated from world class leaders from Europe, given their interests in America's highly skilled labor force and first-class university infrastructure. Most of this investment took place among European firms in such research-intensive sectors as chemicals, telecommunications, and automobiles.

5. Intra-Firm Trade of Foreign Affiliates

While we have frequently highlighted the fact that cross-border trade is a secondary means of delivery goods and services across the Atlantic, the modes of delivery—affiliate sales and trade—should not be viewed independently. They are more complements than substitutes, since foreign investment and affiliate sales increasingly drive cross-border trade flows. Indeed, a substantial share of transatlantic trade is considered intra-firm trade or related party trade, which is cross-border trade that stays within the ambit of the company.

For instance, it's related party trade when BMW or Mercedes of Germany sends parts to BMW of South Carolina or Mercedes of Alabama, or when Lafarge or Michelin sends intermediate components to its plants in the Greater Cincinnati area, or when 3M ships components for its office products or communications sectors from St. Paul to affiliates in Germany or UK. The tight linkages between European parent companies and their

U.S. affiliates is reflected in the fact roughly 58% of U.S. imports from the European Union consisted of related party trade in 2005. The percentage was even higher in the case of Ireland (89.3%) and Germany (61.5%). Meanwhile, roughly 32% of U.S. exports to Europe in 2004 represented related party trade. It helps to explain why tiny Ireland is the number one export destination for such U.S. states as Minnesota, Washington, Maine or New Mexico: each hosts companies engaged in close intra-firm trade with the Celtic Tiger.

Against this backdrop, it is hardly surprising that the U.S. dollar's long-term decline against the euro since 2002 has done little to correct America's rather large trade deficit with Europe. Following such a large shift in prices or exchange rates, Economics 101 would predict a rebalancing of bilateral trade. Economic theory would expect a gradual improvement in the overall trade balance. In fact, however, the opposite has occurred: America's trade deficit (in goods and services) with the European Union actually widened again in 2005, to $98 billion, up over 12% from the prior year.

In the end, what is missing from the debate over trade and missing from conventional analysis is the fact that an unusually large percentage of U.S. imports from Europe is considered related party trade, or trade between a parent and an affiliate. Parent-affiliate trade is less responsive to shifts in prices of exchange rates and more attuned to domestic demand. Accordingly, while a strong euro, in theory at least, would be associated with a decline in European competitiveness in the U.S., the fact that many European multinationals produce, market, and distribute goods on both sides of the ocean gives firms a high degree of immunity to a dramatic shift in exchange rates.

Related Party Trade, 2005

	US Imports: "Related Party Trade," as % of Total	US Exports: "Related Party Trade," as % of Total
European Union	57.9	31.7
France	48.7	34.7
Germany	61.5	31.7
Netherlands	57.9	38.7
United Kingdom	58.4	29.5
Other European Union	48.5	28.4

Source: U.S. Census Bureau

6. Foreign Affiliate Sales

U.S. foreign affiliate sales (goods and services) hit a record $3.8 trillion in 2004, well in excess of U.S. exports of $1.2 trillion. Europe accounted for half of total global foreign affiliate sales, with sales totaling $1.9 trillion, up from $1.6 trillion the prior year. Reflecting just how important Europe is to corporate America, sale of U.S. affiliates in Europe were more than double comparable sales in the entire Asia/Pacific region.

Affiliate sales in the United Kingdom ($465 billion) exceeded aggregate sales in Latin America.

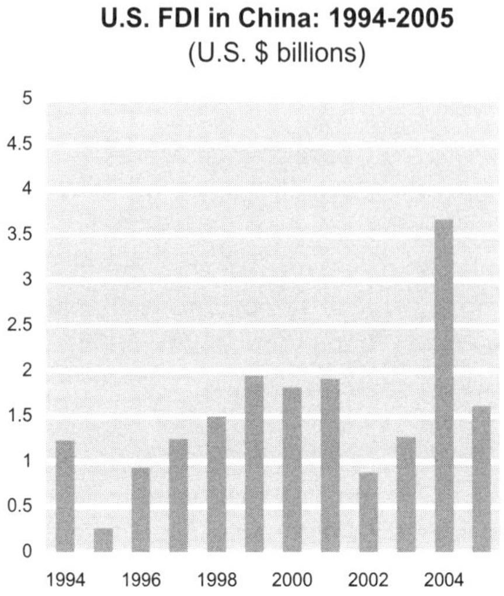

Source: Bureau of Economic Analysis

While U.S. affiliate sales in China have soared over the past decade, they do so from a low base, and still remain well below comparable sales in Europe. For instance, U.S. affiliate sales of $71 billion in China in 2004 were less than affiliate sales in Belgium ($80 billion) and Spain ($78 billion) and well below those in Germany ($286 billion) or France ($176 billion).

Affiliate sales are also the primary means by which European firms deliver goods and services to consumers in the United States. In 2004, for instance, majority-owned European affiliates sales in the U.S. ($1.4 trillion) were more than three times larger than U.S. imports from Europe ($386 billion). In the case of Germany, foreign affiliate sales in the United States totaled $320 billion in 2004, more than triple U.S. imports from Germany the same year ($101 billion). For virtually all nations in Europe, foreign affiliate sales were easily in excess of their U.S. imports in 2004.

7. Foreign Affiliate Profits

The transatlantic profits boom continued in 2004 and in subsequent years. U.S. affiliates in Europe earned a record $98 billion in 2004, nearly double the cyclical low of 2001, when slow growth on both sides of the Atlantic resulted in a transatlantic profits downturn. In 2005, affiliate income surged to $106 billion. Europe remains the most profitable region of the world for U.S. multinationals, with Europe accounting for nearly half of total global affiliate earnings in 2004 and for 53% of the global total over the first half of this decade.

Just how important Europe is to the global earnings of U.S. multinationals is reflected by the following: in 2004, U.S. affiliate income from Europe was nearly three times as large as total earnings from Latin America and double affiliate earnings from Asia. Behind the surge in profits: the steep slide of the U.S. dollar against the pound, euro, and Swiss franc since 2002, which has helped inflate dollar-based earnings of U.S. affiliates in Europe. Lately, a rebound in final demand in Europe has helped drive the earnings of affiliates.

In 2005, a number of countries in Europe—including Austria, Germany, Ireland, Italy, and Portugal to name a few—provided record earnings to U.S. affiliates. U.S. companies also posted strong earning grains from central Europe, in such markets as Poland, the Czech Republic and Hungary. The United Kingdom and the Netherlands, however, rank as the most important markets in the world for corporate America with it comes to global earnings. On average, the Netherlands represented nearly 10.6% and the UK 10.4% of total affiliate income in the first half of this decade.

Similarly, the United States remains the most important market in the world in terms of earnings for many European multinationals. Profits of European foreign affiliates in the United States totaled $62.5 billion in 2004 and rose to $77 billion in 2005. Affiliate earnings were driven largely by strong U.S. demand, which offset the adverse price effect from the long-term strength of the euro and British pound. Strong economic growth in the United States has been also been a key catalyst in boosting corporate profits in Europe, which in turn have helped to promote more investment and employment across the continent. The sectors most exposed to the U.S. market include telecoms, automobiles, media, technology, capital goods, utilities, financial services and pharmaceuticals.

In the end, these seven indices convey a more complete and complex picture of global engagement than simple tallies of exports and imports. Foreign direct investment and foreign affiliate sales, not trade, represent the backbone of the transatlantic economy. The seven variables just highlighted underscore the depth and breadth of U.S.-European bilateral relations.

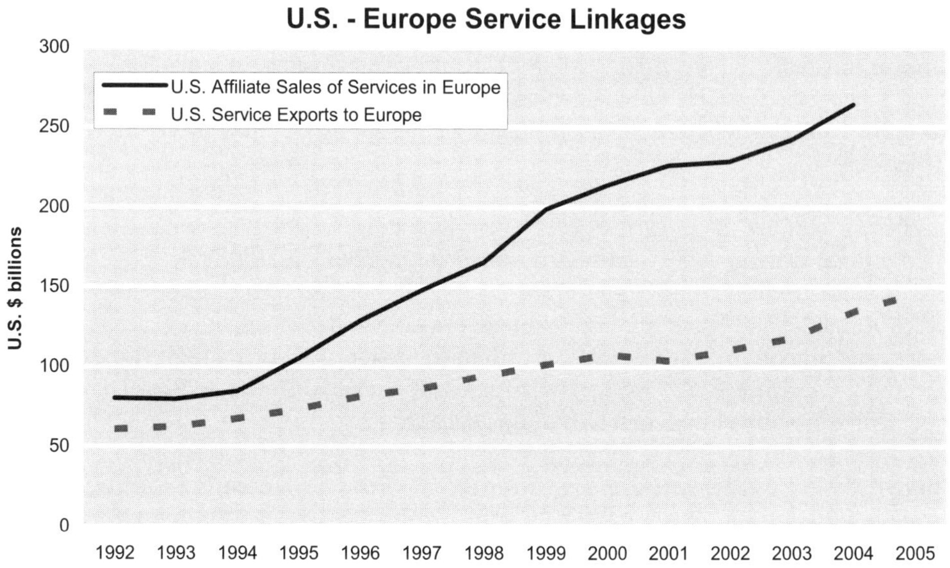

Source: Bureau of Economic Analysis

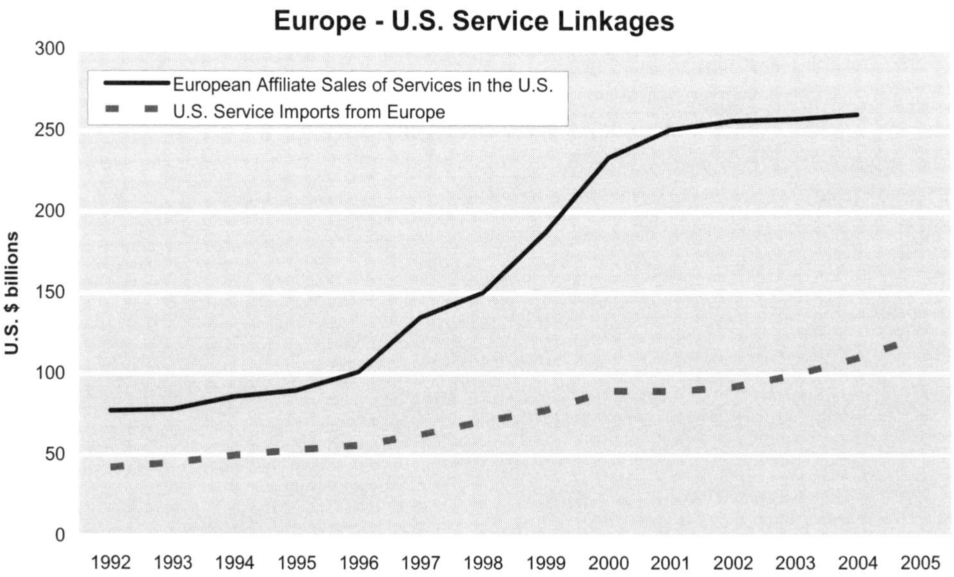

Source: Bureau of Economic Analysis

America's FDI Roots in Europe

($ billions)

Industry	US FDI to Europe	% of Industry Total
European Total	1,059.4	51.2%
Mining	25.6	22.4%
Manufacturing	233.6	51.8%
Food	19.1	60.6%
Chemicals	68.0	62.1%
Primary and fabricated metals	10.0	46.1%
Machinery	15.3	52.4%
Computers and electronic products	27.6	46.9%
Electrical equipment, appliances, and components	7.2	55.0%
Transportation equipment	20.7	42.3%
Wholesale trade	86.8	60.7%
Information	33.5	60.4%
Depository institutions	39.0	55.5%
Finance (except depository institutions) and insurance	176.8	44.9%
Professional, scientific, and technical services	33.1	60.9%
Other industries	263.1	60.0%

Europe's FDI Roots in the US

($ billions)

Industry	US FDI from Europe	% of Industry Total
Total from Europe	1,143.6	70.0%
Manufacturing	414.9	77.1%
Food	15.7	79.3%
Chemicals	136.0	89.7%
Primary and fabricated metals	20.2	70.0%
Machinery	30.7	63.0%
Computers and electronic products	28.5	60.6%
Electrical equipment, appliances, and components	10.6	74.6%
Transportation equipment	44.6	58.7%
Wholesale trade	124.3	54.0%
Retail trade	16.6	55.9%
Information	110.0	77.1%
Depository institutions	98.5	75.2%
Finance (except depository institutions) and insurance	130.4	62.8%
Real estate and rental and leasing	20.6	50.2%
Professional, scientific, and technical services	37.1	88.5%
Other industries	191.6	70.0%

Note: Historic-cost basis, 2005

Source: Bureau of Economic Analysis

The U.S. Earnings Boost from Europe

(U.S. foreign affiliate income from Europe)

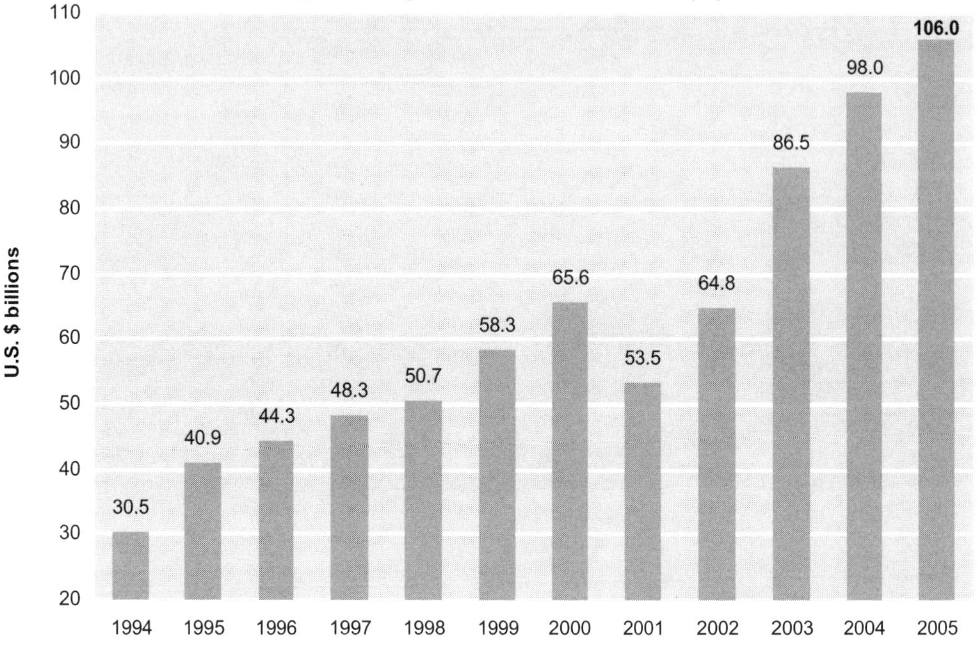

Source: Bureau of Economic Analysis

Chapter 3
European Commerce and the 50 States—A State-by-State Comparison

A Sizable U.S. Footprint

Europe's investment footprint in the United States is quite large and geographically diverse. On a historic cost basis, Europe's investment stakes in the United States topped $1.1 trillion in 2005, more than triple the level of 1995. No other region of the world has made such a large capital commitment to the U.S than Europe, with the latter accounting for nearly 70% of total U.S. inward investment stock in 2005.

Despite transatlantic tensions over the U.S.-led war in Iraq, and notwithstanding growing European investment in other parts of the world, notably central Europe and China, the United States remains among the most attractive foreign markets in the world to European firms. Strong real economic growth, together with a wealthy consumer base, a first-class knowledge economy, and a deep and liquid capital markets remain key endowments of the United States and key attractions to foreign investors.

European Investors in the United States: Regional, Industry, and State Preferences

European investment can be found in all fifty U.S. states. What's more, in many states, including such key states as Michigan, New York, North Carolina, and Texas, European investors lead the way in terms of foreign direct investment, creating new jobs, new sources of income, and new export opportunities in the process.

On a geographic basis, European multinationals continue to show a clear bias towards the Southeast, a function of the region's non-union labor base, low costs, state tax incentives, and first-class infrastructure. On account of these attributes, the Southeast accounted for just over 22% of total European investment in the United States in 2005 (as measured as the stock of gross property, plant and equipment held by European foreign affiliates in the United States). That is down slightly from our last survey. The Great Lakes and Mid-Atlantic states ranked second and third, respectively. At the other end of the spectrum, the Plains states attracted less than 5% of total European investment in the U.S. in 2005.

European Foreign Investment in the U.S.
By geographic region, 2004

Region	U.S. $ billions	% of Total European Investment
Southeast	124.1	22.6
Great Lakes	102.0	18.6
Mid-Atlantic	98.5	18.0
Southwest	69.4	12.6
West	62.2	11.3
New England	36.3	6.6
Rocky Mountains	30.5	5.6
Plains	25.5	4.6

Source: Bureau of Economic Analysis

It is interesting to note that British, French and German foreign investors each favor a different geographic region of thc United States. For instance, the Southeast was the favored location of French firms in 2005; the Great Lakes was the top region for German firms, given the strong links between German automotive firms and Michigan; and the Mid-Atlantic slightly outranked the Southeast as the top geographic investment location for British firms. Swiss investment in the United State is clustered around the Mid-Atlantic states, notably New Jersey and New York. This reflects the large capital position of Swiss pharmaceutical firms in New Jersey and the extensive presence of Swiss financial service firms in New York.

By sector, European investment ties in the U.S. are quite extensive. In manufacturing, the focus is on automotives, chemicals and pulp and paper. Banking, insurance, and hotels are key service areas where European investors have been active in the United States.

Unchanged from the last survey, Texas and California remain the two most attractive states for European investors. Again in 2004, Texas comfortably edged out California as the top U.S. state for European investment, with European investment in Texas totaling \$55.3 billion versus European investment of \$45.1 billion in California. New York ranked third (\$39.1 billion). Europe's investment stakes in Texas largely reflect capital outlays in the state's energy sector. British firms ranked as the top foreign investor in Texas in 2004.

Gross Property, Plant, and Equipment of British Affiliates in U.S. Regions, 2004
(millions of dollars)

Mideast	25,560
Southeast	25,444
Far West	23,718
Great Lakes	23,120
Southwest	21,193
New England	13,479
Rocky Mountains	11,270
Plains	5,051
Total	**204,681**

Source: Bureau of Economic Analysis

Overall Direct Employment of British Affiliates in U.S. Regions, 2004
(thousands of employees)

Southeast	188.6
Mideast	182.7
Great Lakes	147.1
Far West	135.1
Southwest	93.4
New England	91.7
Plains	46.8
Rocky Mountains	30.6
Total	**920.8**

Source: Bureau of Economic Analysis

Manufacturing Employment of British Affiliates in U.S. Regions, 2004
(thousands of employees)

Great Lakes	53.4
Southeast	52.9
Mideast	35.9
Far West	27.0
Southwest	22.4
New England	18.5
Plains	12.4
Rocky Mountains	3.9
Total	**227.5**

Source: Bureau of Economic Analysis

Gross Property, Plant, and Equipment of French Affiliates in U.S. Regions, 2004
(millions of dollars)

Southeast	18,189
Mideast	15,272
Southwest	8,517
Far West	7,335
Great Lakes	7,102
New England	5,011
Plains	3,503
Rocky Mountains	608
Total	**67,787**

Source: Bureau of Economic Analysis

Overall Direct Employment of French Affiliates in U.S. Regions, 2004
(thousands of employees)

Mideast	108.7
Southeast	101.1
Far West:	64.2
Great Lakes:	62.8
Southwest	48.0
New England	30.8
Plains	21.7
Rocky Mountains	13.6
Total	**451.6**

Source: Bureau of Economic Analysis

Manufacturing Employment of French Affiliates in U.S. Regions, 2004
(thousands of employees)

Southeast	43.1
Mideast	24.9
Great Lakes	20.9
Southwest	16.3
Far West	13.8
New England	9.7
Plains	7.3
Rocky Mountains	1.2
Total	**137.4**

Source: Bureau of Economic Analysis

Gross Property, Plant, and Equipment of German Affiliates in U.S. Regions, 2004
(millions of dollars)

Great Lakes	50,395
Southeast	38,131
Mideast	26,459
Southwest	13,939
Far West	11,640
Plains	8,320
New England	5,489
Rocky Mountains	932
Total	**203,216**

Source: Bureau of Economic Analysis

Overall Direct Employment of German Affiliates in U.S. Regions, 2004
(thousands of employees)

Great Lakes	187.2
Southeast	147.2
Mideast	137.8
Far West	73.5
New England	41.5
Southwest	36.7
Plains	33.1
Rocky Mountains	8.7
Total	**668.6**

Source: Bureau of Economic Analysis

Manufacturing Employment of German Affiliates in U.S. Regions, 2004
(thousands of employees)

Great Lakes	93.1
Southeast	71.2
Mideast	23.0
New England	16.9
Plains	16.4
Far West	12.5
Southwest	8.7
Rocky Mountains	2.0
Total	**250.4**

Source: Bureau of Economic Analysis

British investors also were the top European investor in California in 2004, with Japanese investors, however, ranked number one overall. The allure of California is its large and wealthy consumer market, as well as its technological endowments, educational facilities, and agricultural capabilities. These factors are among the key variables behind the $45 billion in European investment in California. Total European investment in California, as in Texas, is greater than total European investment in most nations. This is not surprising given that California's economy is larger than most member states of the European Union. European affiliates are significant employers in the states, directly supporting 337,400 California workers with roughly one-quarter of these jobs in manufacturing activities, a decrease in jobs from 363,300 in 2003. California was a top investment target for British, Swiss, and Dutch firms. In 2004, European affiliates created 67,300 manufacturing jobs in California, higher than in any other state.

Transportation-related Exports from Alabama and South Carolina to Europe
($ millions)

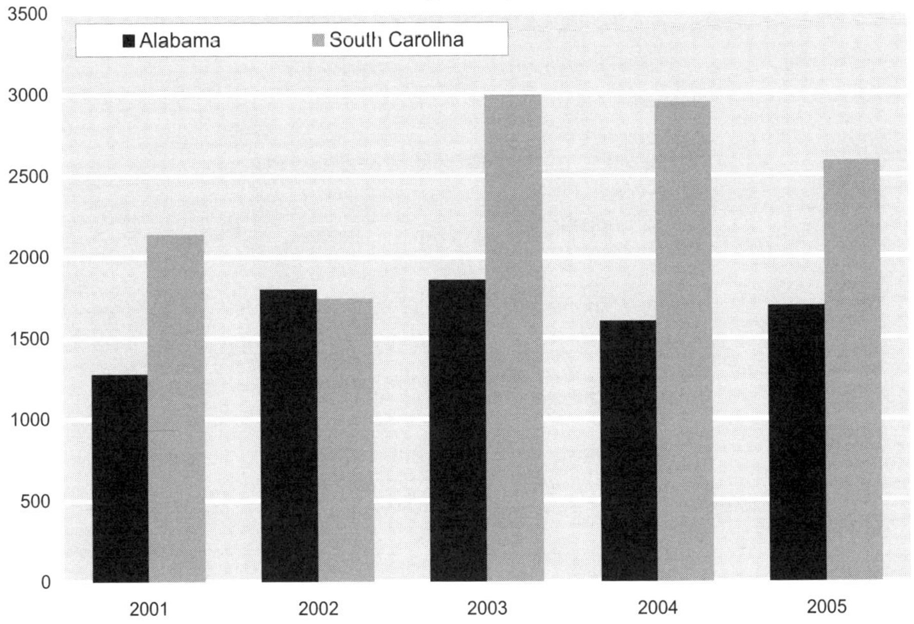

Source: U.S. Department of Commerce

Ranking of U.S. States Benefiting from European Investment

Ranking of States for European Direct Investment
($ billions, 2004)

U.S. State	European Direct Investment (FDI)
Texas	55.3
California	45.1
New York	39.1
Michigan	29.8
New Jersey	25.0
Pennsylvania	22.3
Illinois	21.9
Indiana	20.1
Ohio	18.5
Massachusetts	17.1
North Carolina	16.6
South Carolina	15.9
Kentucky	14.4
Louisiana	13.3
Georgia	13.0
Florida	12.4
Virginia	12.3
Wisconsin	11.7
Missouri	11.3
Alabama	10.4
Utah	10.4
Connecticut	9.6
Washington	9.1
Wyoming	8.7
Tennessee	8.5
Colorado	8.4
Maryland	7.1
Oregon	5.9
Oklahoma	5.8
Minnesota	5.3
Arizona	5.2
Kansas	3.8
Iowa	3.8
West Virginia	3.7
New Hampshire	3.6
Mississippi	3.6
Delaware	3.4
New Mexico	2.9
Rhode Island	2.6
Maine	2.3
Idaho	1.7
Nevada	1.6
Montana	1.4
Vermont	1.1
Nebraska	0.9
Hawaii	0.5
South Dakota	0.3
Alaska	N/A
Arkansas	N/A
North Dakota	N/A

Ranking of States for Jobs Supported Directly by European Investment
(Thousands of employees, 2004)

U.S. State	Employees
California	337.4
New York	289.4
Texas	228.5
Pennsylvania	173.2
New Jersey	170.3
Illinois	167.3
Florida	158.4
North Carolina	158.2
Michigan	145.9
Massachusetts	137.9
Ohio	128.9
Georgia	117.2
Virginia	99.0
South Carolina	94.9
Maryland	85.2
Indiana	84.8
Connecticut	83.9
Tennessee	70.8
Wisconsin	63.6
Missouri	59.9
Minnesota	51.8
Washington	48.8
Alabama	46.7
Kentucky	45.3
Colorado	44.0
Arizona	40.0
Oregon	32.6
New Hampshire	32.3
Louisiana	31.8
Iowa	25.8
Utah	24.8
Kansas	23.3
Arkansas	22.7
Rhode Island	22.2
Maine	21.2
Oklahoma	20.2
Delaware	19.8
Nevada	15.6
Mississippi	14.4
West Virginia	13.0
Nebraska	12.4
Idaho	10.7
Vermont	8.8
Hawaii	8.0
New Mexico	7.8
Wyoming	6.1
Alaska	5.0
Montana	4.5
South Dakota	2.7
North Dakota	N/A

Source: Bureau of Economic Analysis

Trade Linkages: European Multinationals and American States

Virtually every U.S. state benefits from European foreign direct investment, with European foreign affiliates across the United States acting not only as key providers of goods and services to U.S. consumers but also as critical sources of employment. In addition, Europe is also a key export market for many U.S. states, a role that grants even more economic benefits to states, ranging from income growth to the creation of jobs.

California alone exported more than $23 billion in goods to Europe in 2004. Europe is one of the largest world markets for information technology, and technology firms in California and other states, like New York, Colorado and Oregon, have sharply expanded their exports of computers and related parts to Europe over the past few years. Texas and New York are also sizable exporters to Europe. Texas' exports to Europe totaled $13 billion in 2004, while New York exports to Europe were only slightly lower, $12.9 billion. The composition of exports runs the gamut—from machinery to chemicals to pulp and paper. The United Kingdom was the top European export market for nineteen states last year. Germany was second, the top European export market for twelve states.

The deep transatlantic linkages forged by investment and trade flows are underscored by the important ties such states as Alabama, Michigan and South Carolina have with European automobile manufacturers. In many cases, trade flows represent "related party" trade, which are trade flows that stay within the ambit of the company. In this respect, European affiliates in the U.S. are significant exporters in their own right. Indeed, U.S. exports of goods shipped by European affiliates totaled $78 billion in 2004. German affiliates accounted for over 41% of total European affiliate exports. Meanwhile, European affiliates in the U.S. are also significant importers, with U.S. imports of goods shipped to U.S.-based European affiliates totaling $151 billion in 2004. In the aggregate, U.S-based affiliates of European companies accounted for roughly 10% of U.S. total trade (exports plus imports) in 2004, underscoring the key role played by affiliates in influencing U.S. trade flows.

Alabama and Europe

Employment, Investment, and Trade Linkages

Employment

European investment in Alabama supported 46,700 jobs in 2004; 38% of the jobs were in manufacturing.

Investment

Of the $16.9 billion invested in Alabama in 2004, 62%, or $10.4 billion came from Europe.

Sources of FDI within Alabama, 2004	
Country	**FDI ($ Millions)**
Japan	2,871
Germany	2,668
France	2,659
United Kingdom	1,996
Canada	1,794

Trade

In 2005, Europe purchased $3.3 billion worth of goods from Alabama.
One half of total exports represented transportation equipment, reflecting the state's linkages with European auto manufacturers.

Top European Export Markets, 2005	
Country	**Exports ($ Millions)**
Germany	1,640
United Kingdom	466
France	273
Netherlands	268
Ireland	147

Top Ten Exports to Europe ($ Millions)

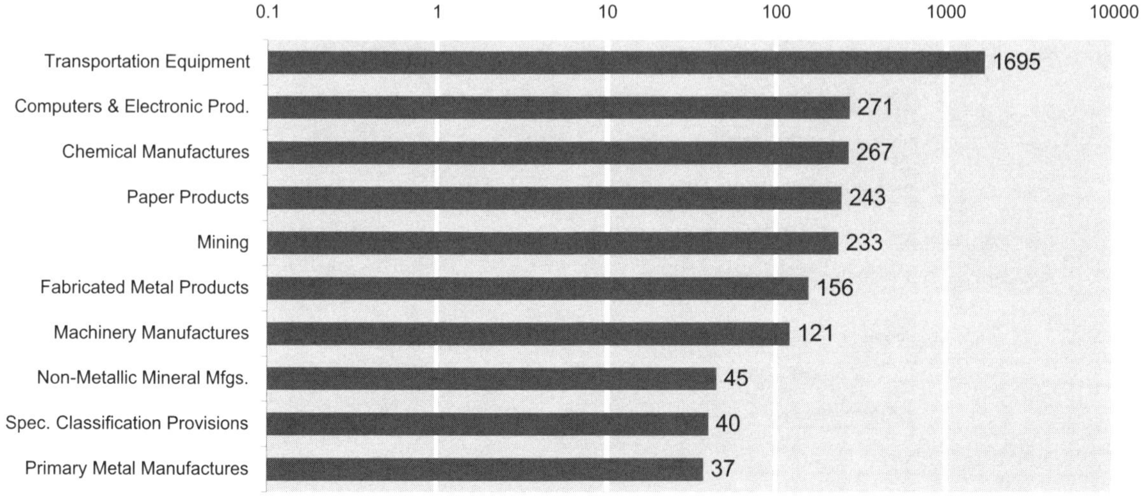

Source: Bureau of Economic Analysis; Office of Trade and Industry Information

Alaska and Europe

Employment, Investment, and Trade Linkages

Employment

European investment in Alaska supported 5,000 jobs in 2004; 4% of the jobs were in manufacturing.

Investment

Alaska receives nearly all of its inward foreign direct investment from Canada and Japan.

Sources of FDI within Alaska, 2004	
Country	**FDI ($ Millions)**
Canada	1,849
Japan	799
Germany	48
Switzerland	29
Netherlands	24

Trade

In 2005, Europe purchased $581 million worth of goods from Alaska.
The bulk of exports from Alaska consists of primary commodities.

Top European Export Markets, 2005	
Country	**Exports ($ Millions)**
Germany	180
Netherlands	114
Switzerland	103
Spain	71
Belgium	38

Top Ten Exports to Europe ($ Millions)

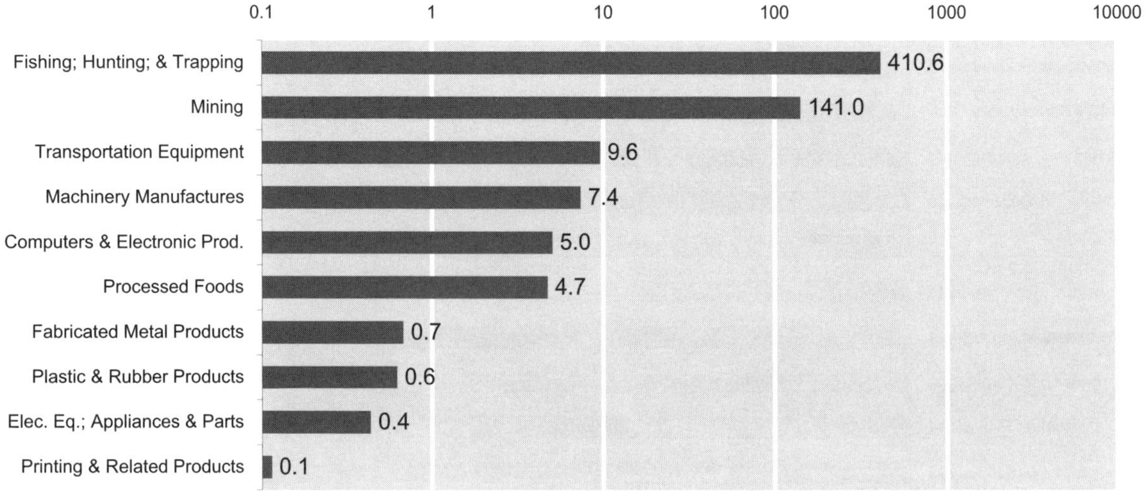

Source: Bureau of Economic Analysis; Office of Trade and Industry Information

Arizona and Europe

Employment, Investment, and Trade Linkages

Employment

European investment in Arizona supported 40,000 jobs in 2004; 16% of the jobs were in manufacturing.

Investment

Of the $9.3 billion invested in Arizona in 2004, 56%, or $5.2 billion came from Europe.

Sources of FDI within Arizona, 2004

Country	FDI ($ Millions)
Germany	1,771
Japan	1,691
United Kingdom	1,341
Canada	825
Switzerland	542

Trade

In 2005, Europe purchased $3.1 billion worth of goods from Arizona.
Nearly 60% of the state's exports consist of transportation equipment and computer/electronic goods.

Top European Export Markets, 2005

Country	Exports ($ Millions)
United Kingdom	761
Germany	743
Netherlands	527
France	441
Switzerland	229

Top Ten Exports to Europe ($ Millions)

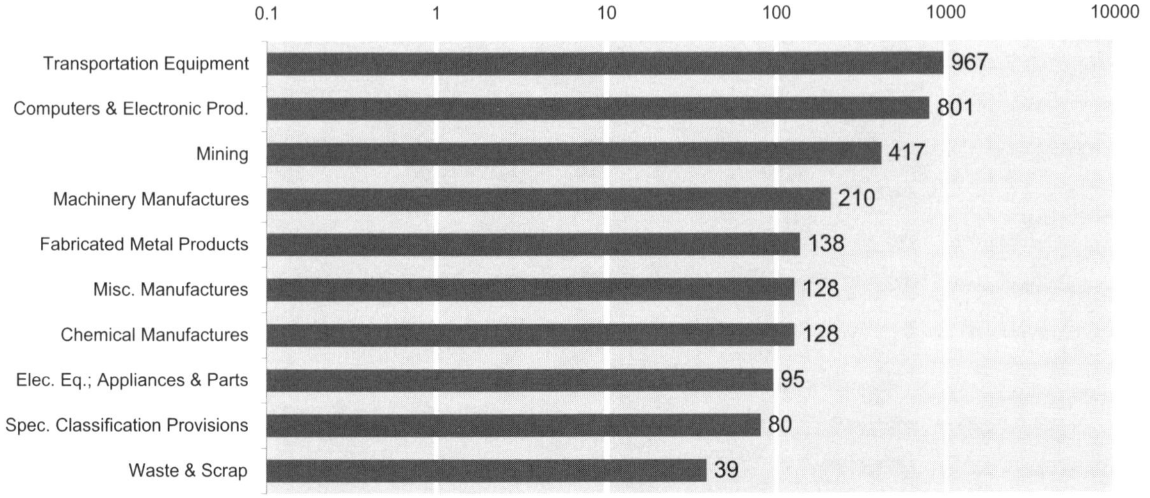

Source: Bureau of Economic Analysis; Office of Trade and Industry Information

Arkansas and Europe

Employment, Investment, and Trade Linkages

Employment

European investment in Arkansas supported 22,700 jobs in 2004; 56% of the jobs were in manufacturing.

Investment

Of the $4.9 billion invested in Arkansas in 2004, over 40% came from Europe.

Sources of FDI within Arkansas, 2004

Country	FDI ($ Millions)
France	732
Japan	535
United Kingdom	404
Switzerland	367
Germany	235

Trade

In 2005, Europe purchased $1.0 billion worth of goods from Arkansas. Transportation equipment was the top export to Europe.

Top European Export Markets, 2005

Country	Exports ($ Millions)
France	270
United Kingdom	191
Portugal	105
Belgium	89
Switzerland	81

Top Ten Exports to Europe ($ Millions)

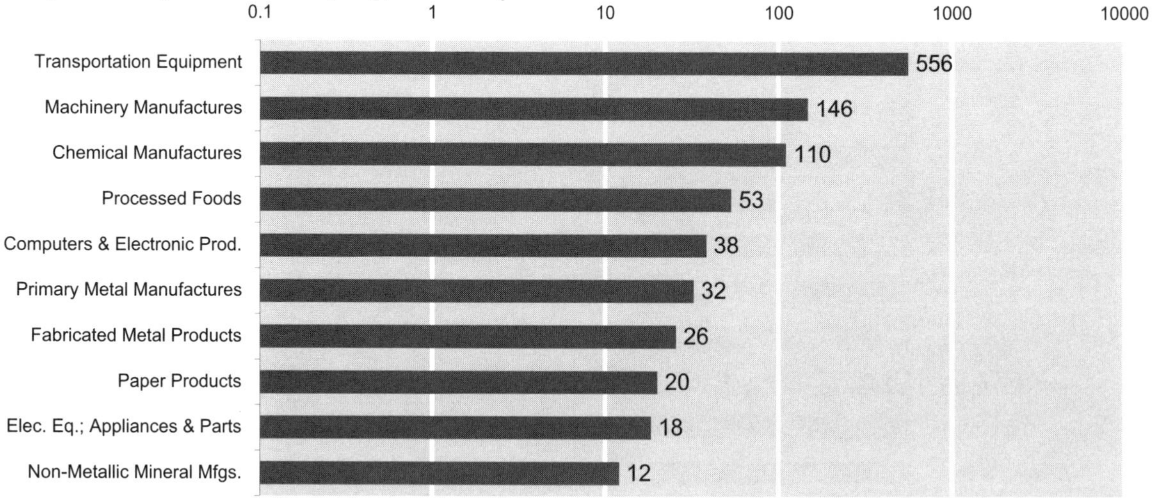

Source: Bureau of Economic Analysis; Office of Trade and Industry Information

California and Europe

Employment, Investment, and Trade Linkages

Employment

European investment in California supported 337,400 jobs in 2004; 20% of the jobs were in manufacturing.

Investment

Of the $90.6 billion invested in California in 2004, 50%, or $45.1 billion came from Europe.

Sources of FDI within California, 2004

Country	FDI ($ Millions)
Japan	20,668
United Kingdom	16,241
Germany	7,000
Australia	6,960
Netherlands	6,544

Trade

In 2005, Europe purchased $23.2 billion worth of goods from California.
More than a third of Californian exports to Europe consists of high-tech goods.

Top European Export Markets, 2005

Country	Exports ($ Millions)
United Kingdom	5,029
Germany	4,266
Netherlands	3,622
France	2,692
Belgium	1,759

Top Ten Exports to Europe ($ Millions)

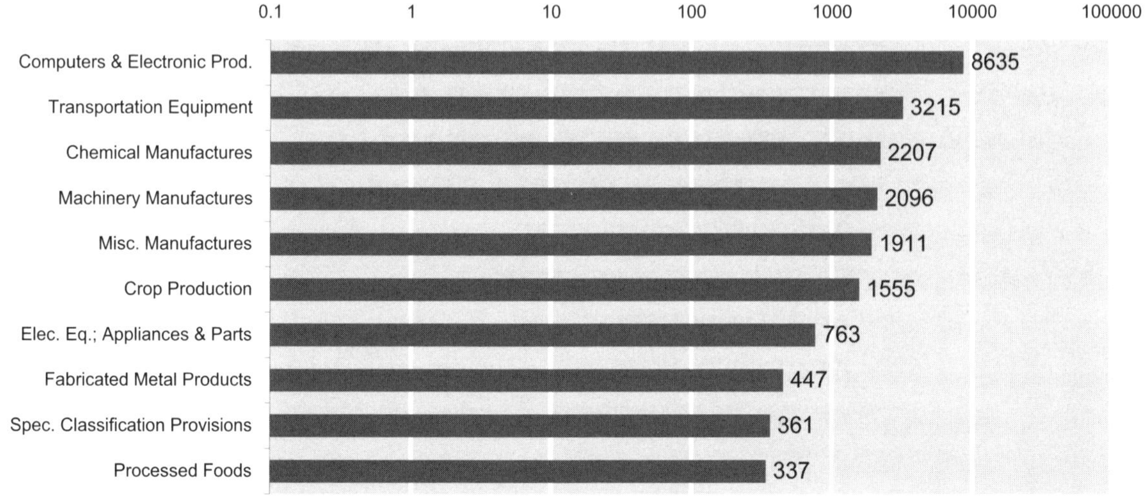

Source: Bureau of Economic Analysis; Office of Trade and Industry Information

Colorado and Europe

Employment, Investment, and Trade Linkages

Employment

European investment in Colorado supported 44,000 jobs in 2004; 20% of the jobs were in manufacturing.

Investment

Of the $16.1 billion invested in Colorado in 2004, 52%, or $8.4 billion came from Europe.

Sources of FDI within Colorado, 2004	
Country	**FDI ($ Millions)**
Canada	5,735
United Kingdom	4,389
Switzerland	1,152
Netherlands	864
France	608

Trade

In 2005, Europe purchased $1.3 billion worth of goods from Colorado.
Over half of the state's exports consist of high-tech goods like computers and electronic products.

Top European Export Markets, 2005	
Country	**Exports ($ Millions)**
Germany	278
Netherlands	244
United Kingdom	241
France	225
Switzerland	79

Top Ten Exports to Europe ($ Millions)

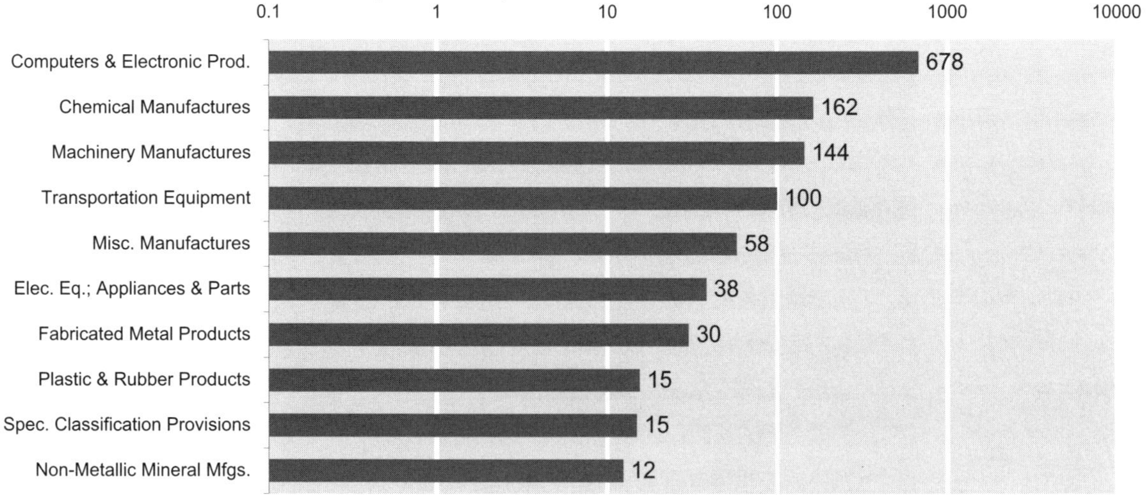

Source: Bureau of Economic Analysis; Office of Trade and Industry Information

Connecticut and Europe

Employment, Investment, and Trade Linkages

Employment

European investment in Connecticut supported 83,900 jobs in 2004; 23% of the jobs were in manufacturing.

Investment

Of the $12.5 billion invested in Connecticut in 2004, 77%, or $9.6 billion came from Europe.

Sources of FDI within Connecticut, 2004

Country	FDI ($ Millions)
Germany	2,466
Netherlands	2,063
United Kingdom	1,910
France	979
Switzerland	856

Trade

In 2005, Europe purchased $4.4 billion worth of goods from Connecticut. Exports are heavily skewed towards transportation equipment.

Top European Export Markets, 2005

Country	Exports ($ Millions)
France	1,602
Germany	832
United Kingdom	697
Netherlands	365
Belgium	263

Top Ten Exports to Europe ($ Millions)

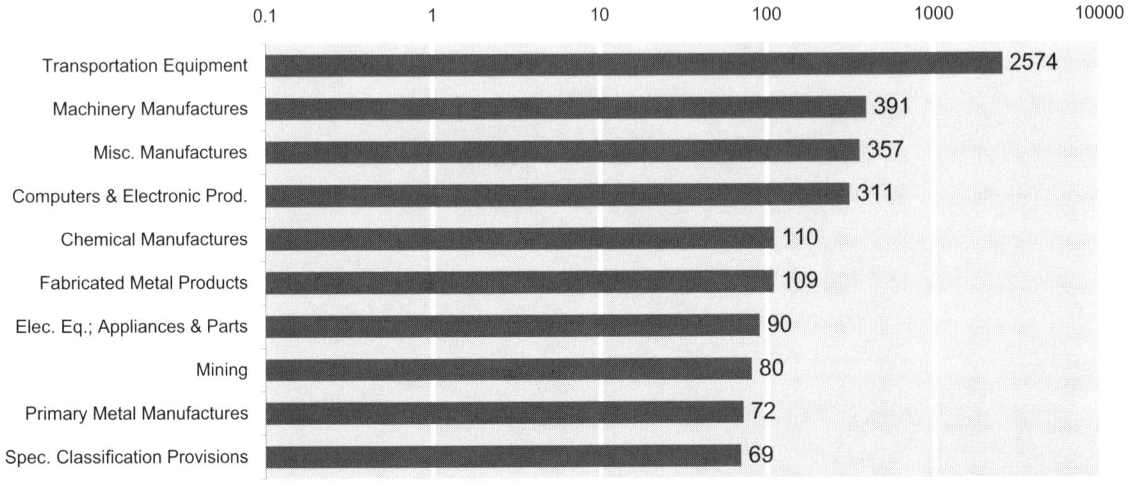

Source: Bureau of Economic Analysis; Office of Trade and Industry Information

Delaware and Europe

Employment, Investment, and Trade Linkages

Employment

European investment in Delaware supported 19,800 jobs in 2004; German and British companies were the largest employers.

Investment

Of the $4.5 billion invested in Delaware in 2004, 76%, or $3.4 billion came from Europe.

Sources of FDI within Delaware, 2004	
Country	**FDI ($ Millions)**
United Kingdom	1,507
Canada	480
France	227
Japan	121
Netherlands	102

Trade

In 2005, Europe purchased $838 million worth of goods from Delaware.
Chemicals are the primary export to Europe.

Top European Export Markets, 2005	
Country	**Exports ($ Millions)**
Germany	287
United Kingdom	263
Belgium	127
Netherlands	80
Italy	21

Top Ten Exports to Europe ($ Millions)

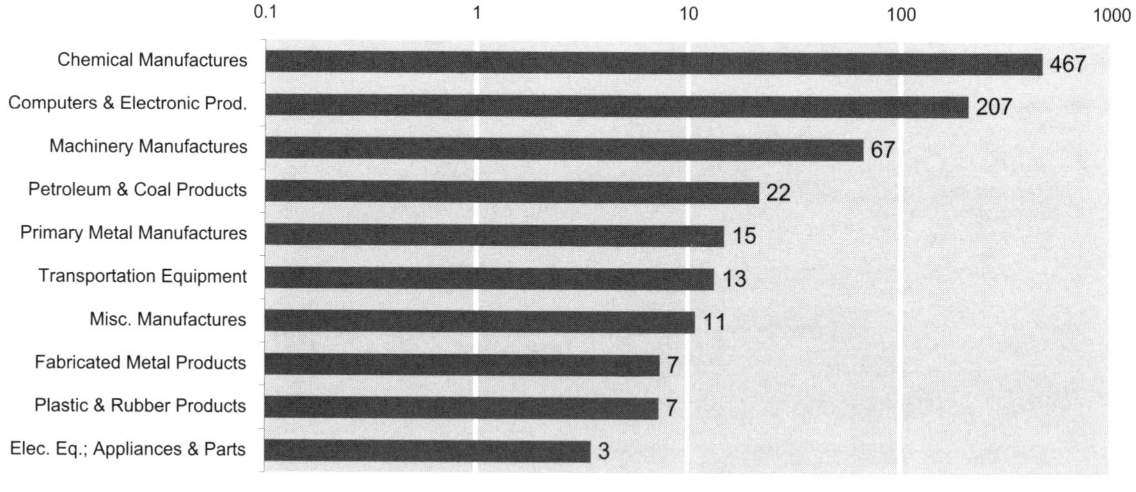

Source: Bureau of Economic Analysis; Office of Trade and Industry Information

Florida and Europe

Employment, Investment, and Trade Linkages

Employment

European investment in Florida supported 158,400 jobs in 2004; 13% of the jobs were in manufacturing.

Investment

Of the $26.8 billion invested in Florida in 2004, 46%, or $12.4 billion came from Europe.

Sources of FDI within Florida, 2004	
Country	**FDI ($ Millions)**
Canada	5,596
United Kingdom	3,754
Germany	2,798
Australia	2,003
Japan	1,993

Trade

In 2005, Europe purchased $4.7 billion worth of goods from Florida.
The state exports a great deal of agricultural goods to the EU, although computers and transportation equipment account for well over half of total exports.

Top European Export Markets, 2005	
Country	**Exports ($ Millions)**
United Kingdom	1,089
Netherlands	789
Germany	762
France	392
Italy	388

Top Ten Exports to Europe ($ Millions)

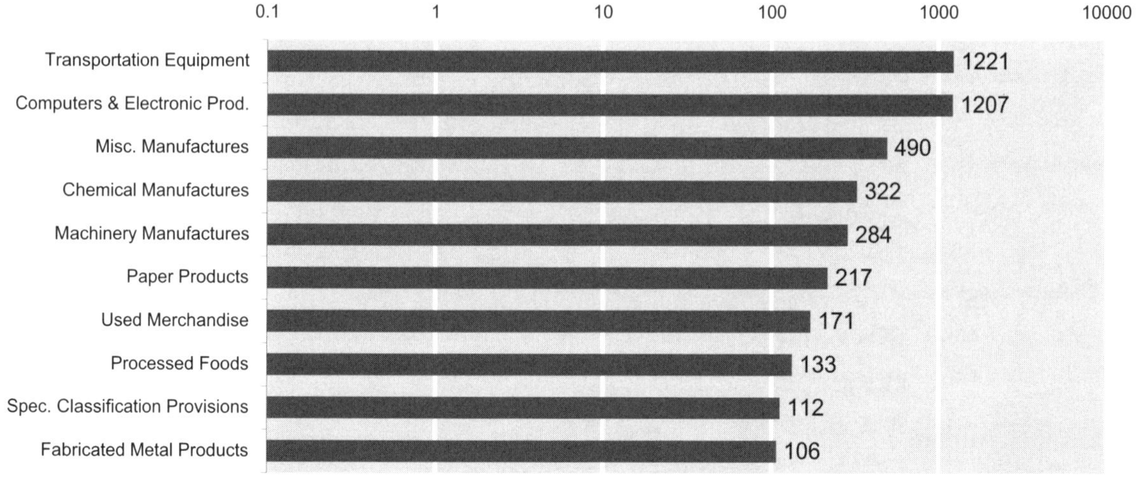

Source: Bureau of Economic Analysis; Office of Trade and Industry Information

Georgia and Europe
Employment, Investment, and Trade Linkages

Employment
European investment in Georgia supported 117,200 jobs in 2004; 26% of the jobs were in manufacturing.

Investment
Of the $23.6 billion invested in Georgia in 2004, 55%, or $13.0 billion came from Europe.

Sources of FDI within Georgia, 2004	
Country	**FDI ($ Millions)**
Japan	4,699
Germany	3,512
United Kingdom	2,576
France	2,399
Canada	1,907

Trade
In 2005, Europe purchased $5.1 billion worth of goods from Georgia.
Exports are broadly diversified among such exports as transportation equipment, chemicals, and computers.

Top European Export Markets, 2005	
Country	**Exports ($ Millions)**
United Kingdom	1,176
Germany	837
Netherlands	761
Italy	555
France	359

Top Ten Exports to Europe ($ Millions)

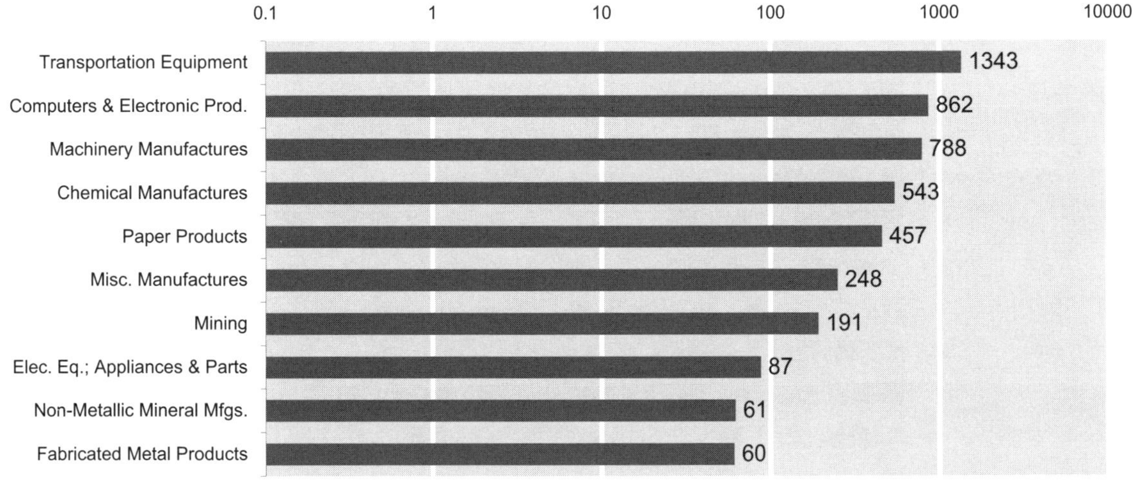

Source: Bureau of Economic Analysis; Office of Trade and Industry Information

Hawaii and Europe

Employment, Investment, and Trade Linkages

Employment

European investment in Hawaii supported 8,000 jobs in 2004; 5% of the jobs were in manufacturing.

Investment

Of the $6.9 billion invested in Hawaii in 2004, 7%, or $468 million came from Europe.

Sources of FDI within Hawaii, 2004	
Country	**FDI ($ Millions)**
Japan	5,840
Germany	149
France	96
Italy	57
Switzerland	56

Trade

In 2005, Europe purchased $28 million worth of goods from Hawaii.
Exports to Europe are small, though heavily weighted towards transportation equipment.

Top European Export Markets, 2005	
Country	**Exports ($ Millions)**
United Kingdom	10
Germany	7
Spain	6
France	2
Netherlands	1

Top Ten Exports to Europe ($ Millions)

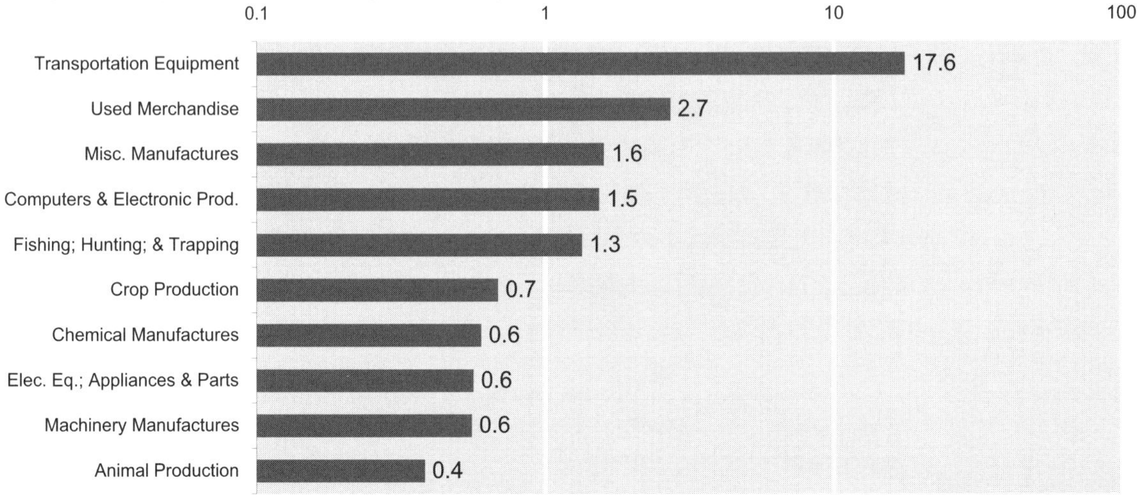

Source: Bureau of Economic Analysis; Office of Trade and Industry Information

Idaho and Europe

Employment, Investment, and Trade Linkages

Employment

European investment in Idaho supported 10,700 jobs in 2004; 37% of the jobs were in manufacturing.

Investment

Of the $2.2 billion invested in Idaho in 2004, 77%, or $1.7 billion came from Europe.

Sources of FDI within Idaho, 2004	
Country	**FDI ($ Millions)**
France	413
Germany	83
Japan	49
Italy	39
Sweden	3

Trade

In 2005, Europe purchased $558 million worth of goods from Idaho.
Exports are concentrated in computers and electronic products.

Top European Export Markets, 2005	
Country	**Exports ($ Millions)**
United Kingdom	348
France	64
Germany	39
Netherlands	34
Italy	29

Top Ten Exports to Europe ($ Millions)

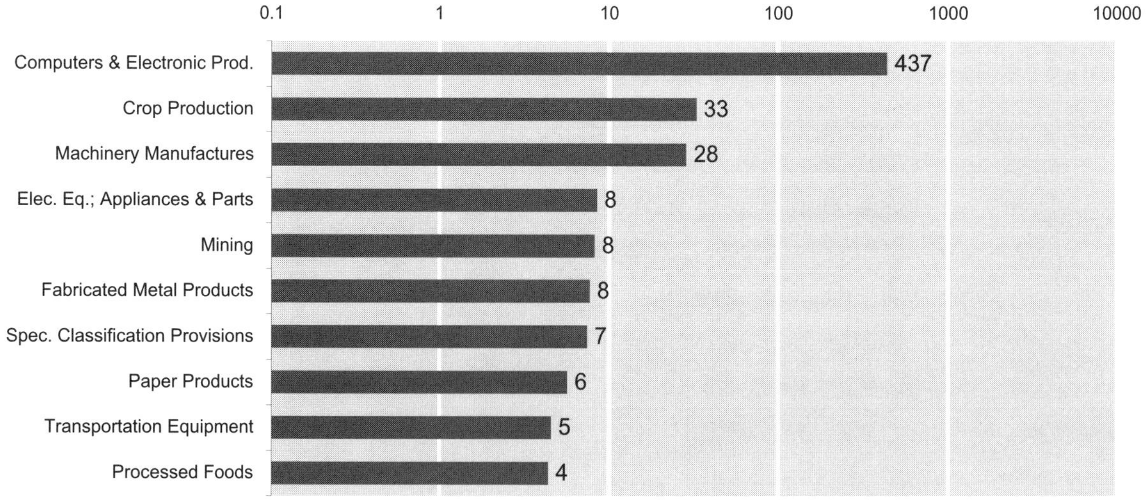

Source: Bureau of Economic Analysis; Office of Trade and Industry Information

Illinois and Europe

Employment, Investment, and Trade Linkages

Employment

European investment in Illinois supported 167,300 jobs in 2004; 25% of the jobs were in manufacturing.

Investment

Of the $39.3 billion invested in Illinois in 2004, 56%, or $21.9 billion came from Europe.

Sources of FDI within Illinois, 2004

Country	FDI ($ Millions)
Japan	8,703
Germany	8,659
United Kingdom	7,966
Canada	958
France	923

Trade

In 2005, Europe purchased $8.5 billion worth of goods from Illinois.
Machinery is a key export to European markets, followed by chemicals and computers.

Top European Export Markets, 2005

Country	Exports ($ Millions)
United Kingdom	1,851
Germany	1,781
Belgium	1,313
Netherlands	1,236
France	835

Top Ten Exports to Europe ($ Millions)

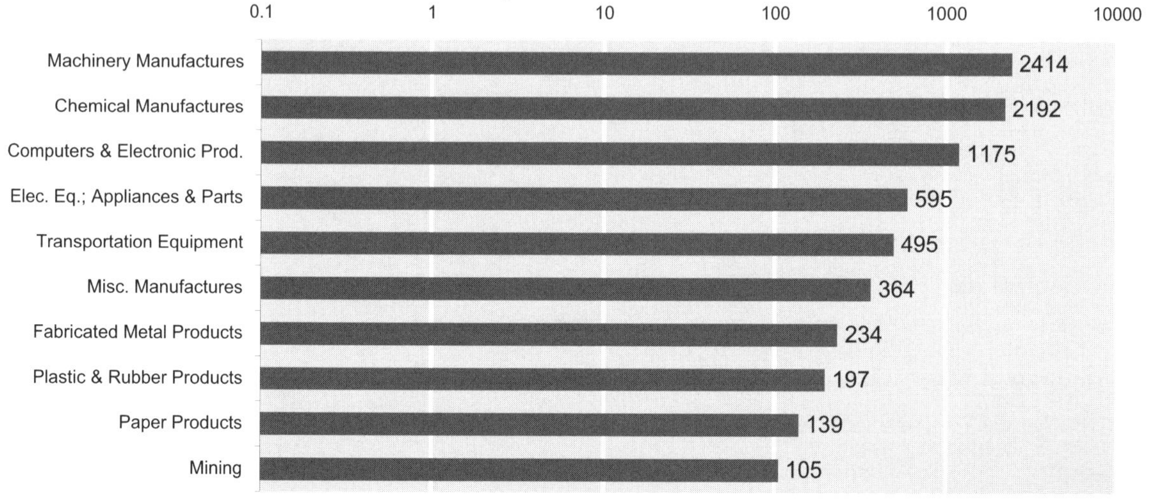

Source: Bureau of Economic Analysis; Office of Trade and Industry Information

Indiana and Europe

Employment, Investment, and Trade Linkages

Employment

European investment in Indiana supported 84,800 jobs in 2004; 56% of the jobs were in manufacturing.

Investment

Of the $30.9 billion invested in Indiana in 2004, 65%, or $20.1 billion came from Europe.

Sources of FDI within Indiana, 2004

Country	FDI ($ Millions)
Japan	7,841
Germany	7,138
United Kingdom	7,004
Canada	4,128
Netherlands	1,870

Trade

In 2005, Europe purchased $5.3 billion worth of goods from Indiana.
Exports are skewed toward chemicals, followed by transportation equipment and manufactures.

Top European Export Markets, 2005

Country	Exports ($ Millions)
United Kingdom	1,516
France	1,467
Germany	691
Netherlands	427
Switzerland	213

Top Ten Exports to Europe ($ Millions)

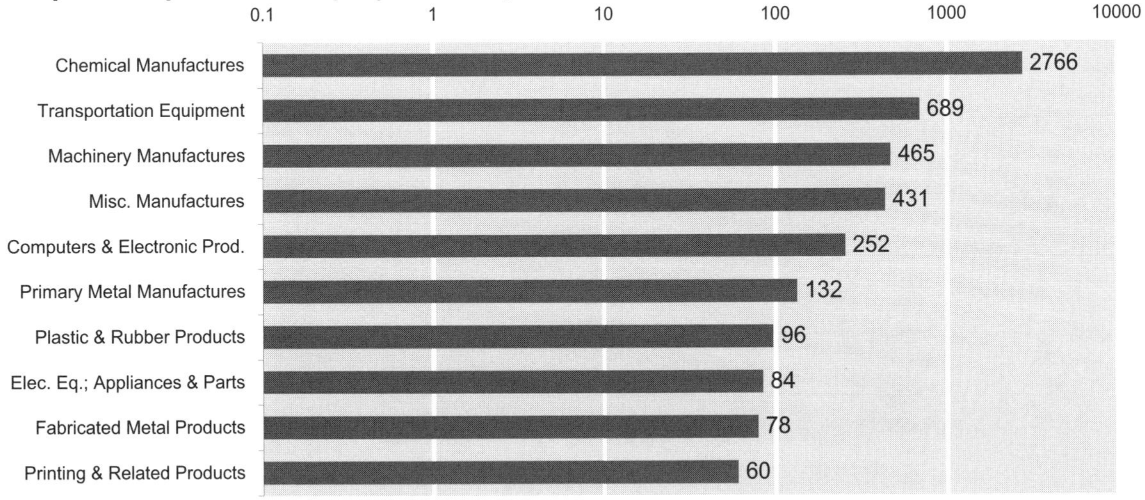

Source: Bureau of Economic Analysis; Office of Trade and Industry Information

Iowa and Europe

Employment, Investment, and Trade Linkages

Employment

European investment in Iowa supported 25,800 jobs in 2004; 46% of the jobs were in manufacturing.

Investment

Of the $6.4 billion invested in Iowa in 2004, 59%, or $3.8 billion came from Europe.

Sources of FDI within Iowa, 2004

Country	FDI ($ Millions)
Canada	1,245
France	885
Germany	845
Japan	681
United Kingdom	565

Trade

In 2005, Europe purchased $1.4 billion worth of goods from Iowa.
The state's exports to the European Union are spread across industries related to machinery and manufactures.

Top European Export Markets, 2005

Country	Exports ($ Millions)
Germany	316
United Kingdom	256
France	231
Netherlands	132
Ireland	102

Top Ten Exports to Europe ($ Millions)

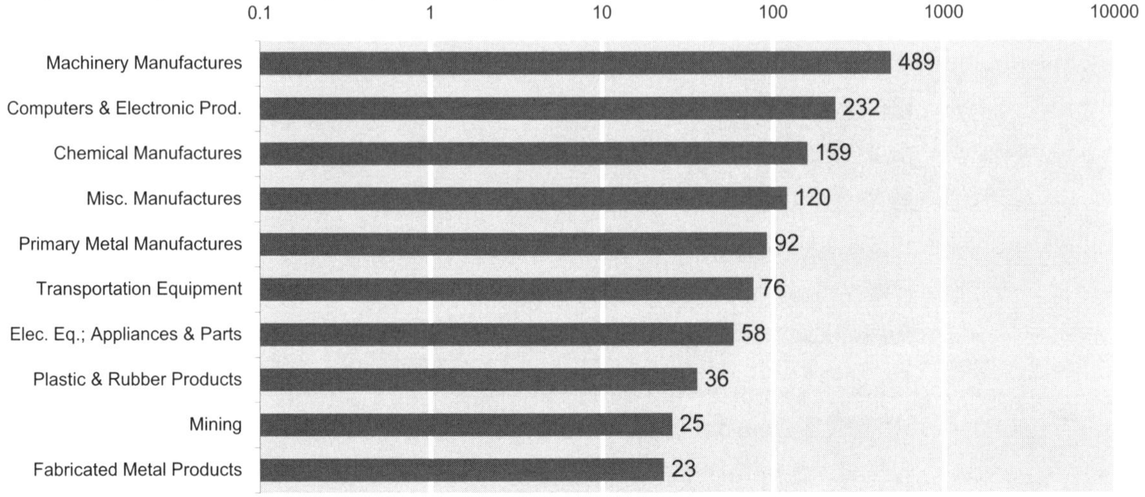

Source: Bureau of Economic Analysis; Office of Trade and Industry Information

Kansas and Europe

Employment, Investment, and Trade Linkages

Employment

European investment in Kansas supported 23,300 jobs in 2004; 36% of the jobs were in manufacturing.

Investment

Of the $5.3 billion invested in Kansas in 2004, 72%, or $3.8 billion came from Europe.

Sources of FDI within Kansas, 2004	
Country	**FDI ($ Millions)**
United Kingdom	1,204
Canada	890
Germany	707
France	596
Netherlands	503

Trade

In 2005, Europe purchased $1.4 billion worth of goods from Kansas.
Nearly half of the state's exports consist of transportation equipment.

Top European Export Markets, 2005	
Country	**Exports ($ Millions)**
United Kingdom	306
Germany	280
France	163
Portugal	125
Italy	108

Top Ten Exports to Europe ($ Millions)

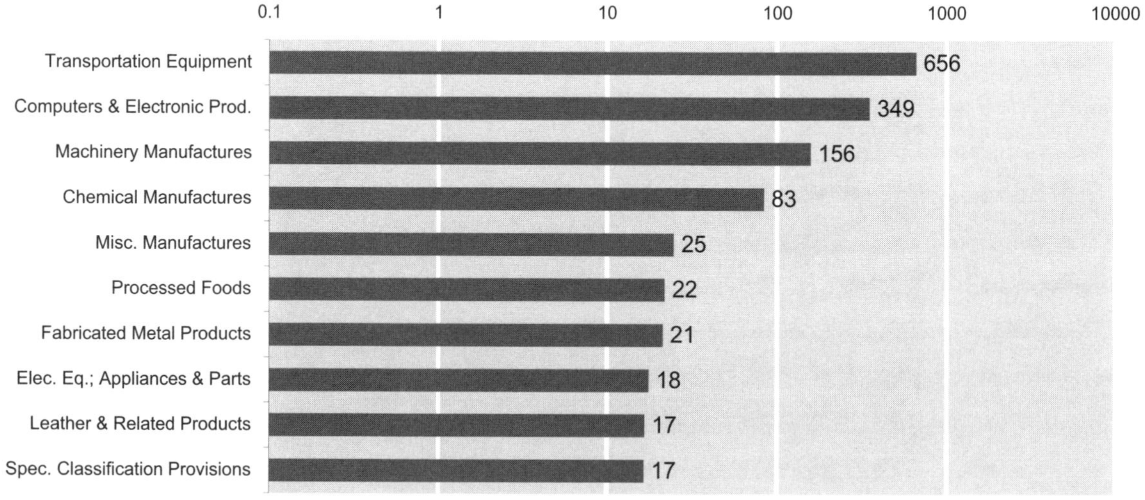

Source: Bureau of Economic Analysis; Office of Trade and Industry Information

Kentucky and Europe

Employment, Investment, and Trade Linkages

Employment

European investment in Kentucky supported 45,300 jobs in 2004; 45% of the jobs were in manufacturing.

Investment

Of the $26.9 billion invested in Kentucky in 2004, 54%, or $14.4 billion came from Europe.

Sources of FDI within Kentucky, 2004	
Country	**FDI ($ Millions)**
Japan	8,850
Germany	8,079
Canada	2,200
France	2,104
United Kingdom	1,003

Trade

In 2005, Europe purchased $4.2 billion worth of goods from Kentucky.
Reflecting the large presence of automobile manufacturers in the state, Kentucky's top export to the European Union is transportation equipment.

Top European Export Markets, 2005	
Country	**Exports ($ Millions)**
France	1,288
United Kingdom	998
Netherlands	508
Germany	458
Belgium	252

Top Ten Exports to Europe ($ Millions)

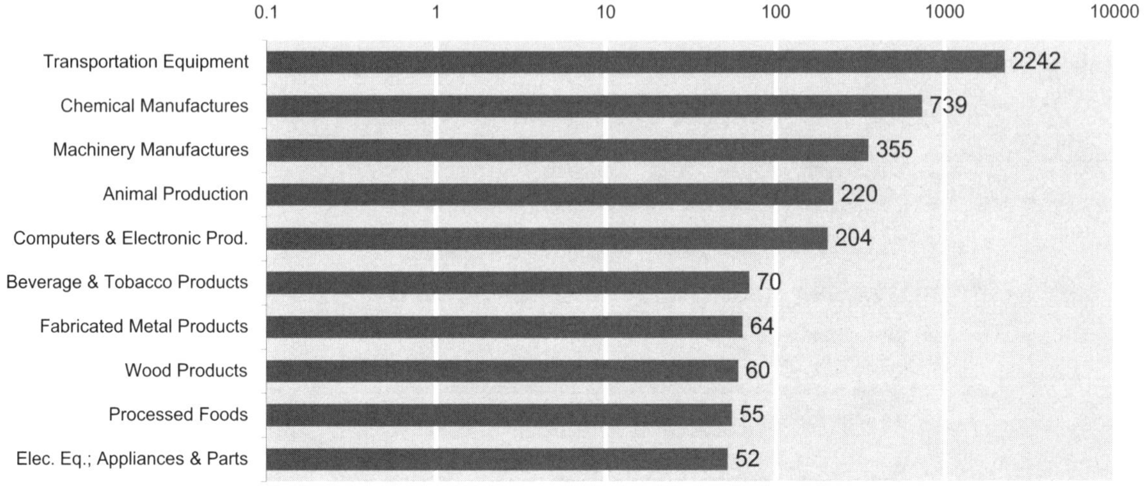

Source: Bureau of Economic Analysis; Office of Trade and Industry Information

Louisiana and Europe

Employment, Investment, and Trade Linkages

Employment

European investment in Louisiana supported 31,800 jobs in 2004; 22% of the jobs were in manufacturing.

Investment

Of the $28.0 billion invested in Louisiana in 2004, 48%, or $13.3 billion came from Europe.

Sources of FDI within Louisiana, 2004	
Country	**FDI ($ Millions)**
Netherlands	4,951
United Kingdom	2,758
Germany	2,671
France	1,670
Canada	1,639

Trade

In 2005, Europe purchased $2.7 billion worth of goods from Louisiana. Chemicals constituted nearly one-third of merchandise exports to Europe.

Top European Export Markets, 2005	
Country	**Exports ($ Millions)**
Netherlands	632
Belgium	471
United Kingdom	340
Germany	333
Spain	216

Top Ten Exports to Europe ($ Millions)

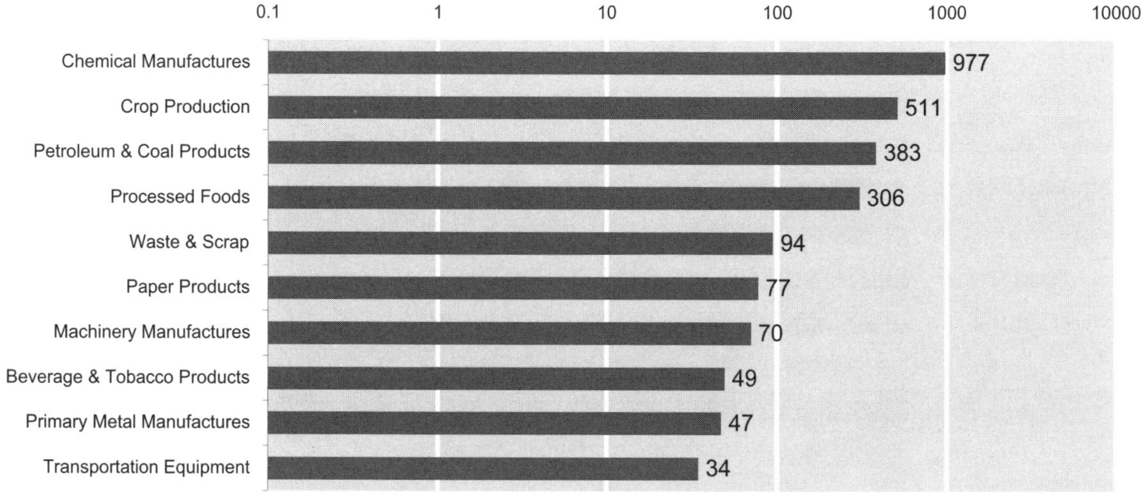

Source: Bureau of Economic Analysis; Office of Trade and Industry Information

Maine and Europe

Employment, Investment, and Trade Linkages

Employment

European investment in Maine supported 21,200 jobs in 2004; 18% of the jobs were in manufacturing.

Investment

Of the $5.3 billion invested in Maine in 2004, 43%, or $2.3 billion came from Europe.

Sources of FDI within Maine, 2004	
Country	**FDI ($ Millions)**
Canada	1,453
United Kingdom	403
Japan	186
Germany	112
France	68

Trade

In 2005, Europe purchased $289 million worth of goods from Maine.
Paper products are the state's top exports to Europe.

Top European Export Markets, 2005	
Country	**Exports ($ Millions)**
Netherlands	50
United Kingdom	47
Belgium	43
Italy	36
Germany	29

Top Ten Exports to Europe ($ Millions)

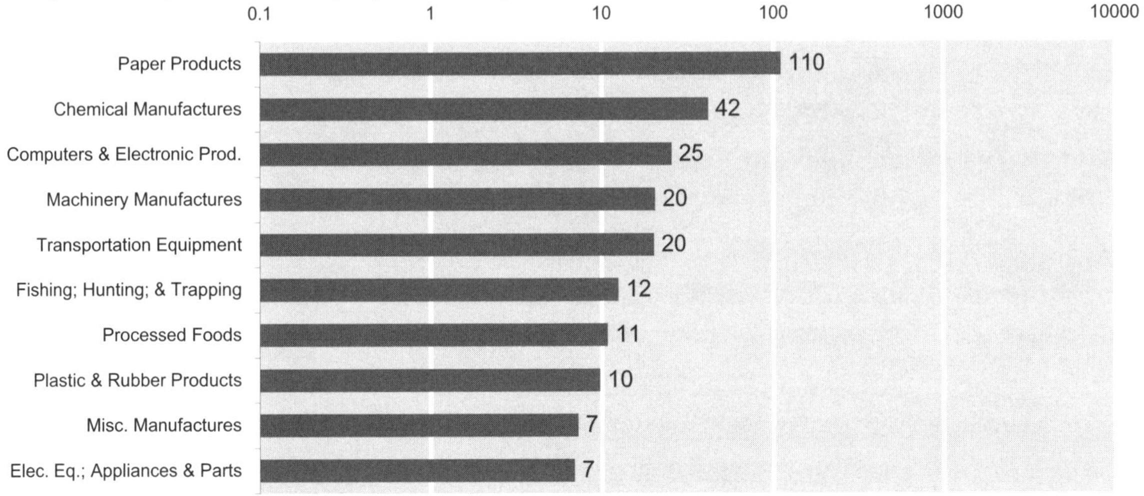

Source: Bureau of Economic Analysis; Office of Trade and Industry Information

Maryland and Europe

Employment, Investment, and Trade Linkages

Employment

European investment in Maryland supported 85,200 jobs in 2004; 12% of the jobs were in manufacturing.

Investment

Of the $11.2 billion invested in Maryland in 2004, 63%, or $7.1 billion came from Europe.

Sources of FDI within Maryland, 2004	
Country	**FDI ($ Millions)**
Netherlands	1,878
Germany	1,385
Japan	1,168
United Kingdom	1,140
Canada	892

Trade

In 2005, Europe purchased $1.9 billion worth of goods from Maryland.
Top exports are chemicals, followed by computers, electronic products and transportation equipment.

Top European Export Markets, 2005	
Country	**Exports ($ Millions)**
Belgium	379
United Kingdom	350
Germany	295
Netherlands	212
Italy	152

Top Ten Exports to Europe ($ Millions)

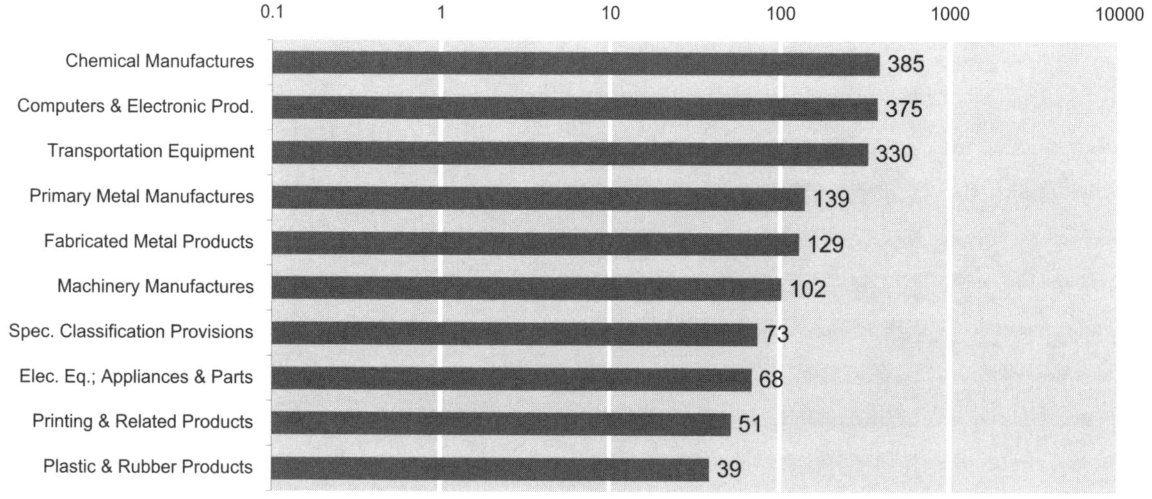

Source: Bureau of Economic Analysis; Office of Trade and Industry Information

Massachusetts and Europe

Employment, Investment, and Trade Linkages

Employment

European investment in Massachusetts supported 137,900 jobs in 2004; 16% of the jobs were in manufacturing.

Investment

Of the $22.8 billion invested in Massachusetts in 2004, 75%, or $17.1 billion came from Europe.

Sources of FDI within Massachusetts, 2004	
Country	**FDI ($ Millions)**
United Kingdom	7,950
France	3,424
Netherlands	2,245
Canada	2,089
Germany	1,698

Trade

In 2005, Europe purchased $9.4 billion worth of goods from Massachusetts.
Exports of chemical manufacturers accounted for more than 40% of exports to Europe

Top European Export Markets, 2005	
Country	**Exports ($ Millions)**
Netherlands	3,002
Germany	2,151
United Kingdom	1,628
France	805
Ireland	447

Top Ten Exports to Europe ($ Millions)

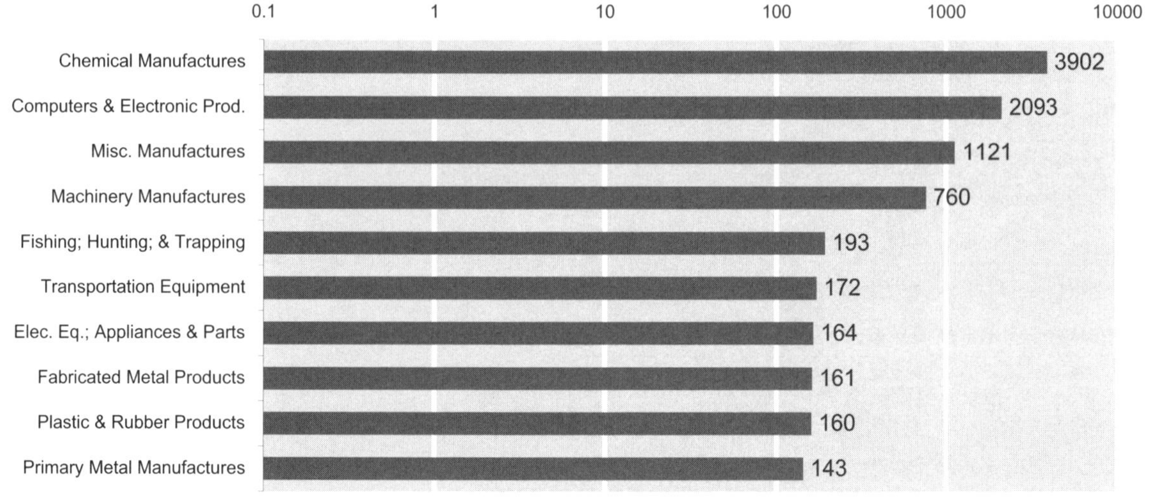

Source: Bureau of Economic Analysis; Office of Trade and Industry Information

Michigan and Europe

Employment, Investment, and Trade Linkages

Employment

European investment in Michigan supported 145,900 jobs in 2004; nearly 40% were in manufacturing.

Investment

Of the $38.9 billion invested in Michigan in 2004, 77%, or $29.8 billion came from Europe.

Sources of FDI within Michigan, 2004	
Country	**FDI ($ Millions)**
Germany	23,742
Japan	4,942
Canada	2,566
France	1,807
United Kingdom	1,563

Trade

In 2005, Europe purchased $4.5 billion worth of goods from Michigan.
Not surprisingly, transportation equipment is Michigan's top export to Europe.

Top European Export Markets, 2005	
Country	**Exports ($ Millions)**
Germany	1,057
United Kingdom	716
Austria	592
France	479
Belgium	443

Top Ten Exports to Europe ($ Millions)

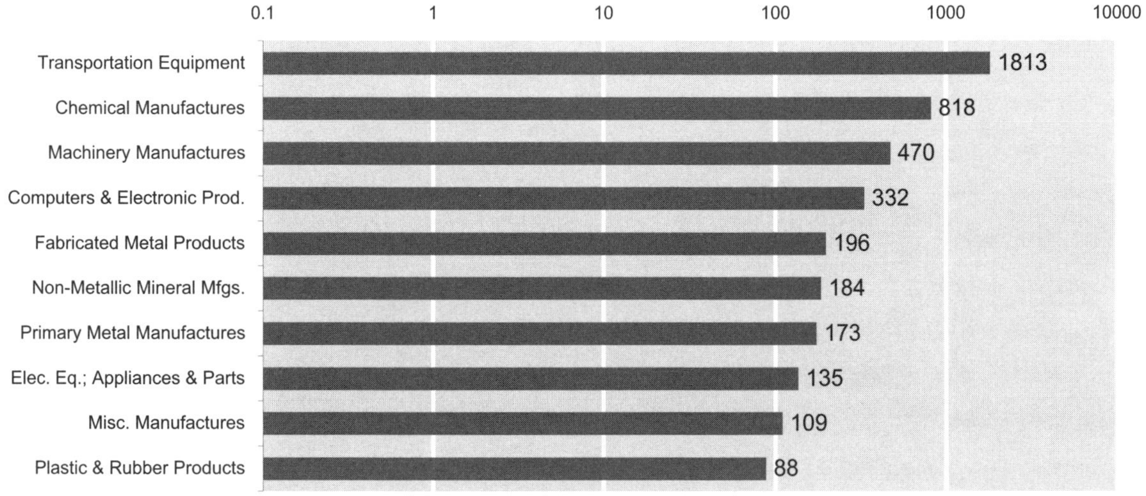

Source: Bureau of Economic Analysis; Office of Trade and Industry Information

Minnesota and Europe

Employment, Investment, and Trade Linkages

Employment

European investment in Minnesota supported 51,800 jobs in 2004; 23% of the jobs were in manufacturing.

Investment

Of the $10.9 billion invested in Minnesota in 2004, 49%, or $5.3 billion came from Europe.

Sources of FDI within Minnesota, 2004

Country	FDI ($ Millions)
Canada	3,540
United Kingdom	1,218
Germany	1,133
France	500
Netherlands	475

Trade

In 2005, Europe purchased $4.9 billion worth of goods from Minnesota.
Miscellaneous manufactures and computers make up more than half of total exports to Europe.

Top European Export Markets, 2005

Country	Exports ($ Millions)
Ireland	1,369
United Kingdom	661
Netherlands	639
Germany	617
France	440

Top Ten Exports to Europe ($ Millions)

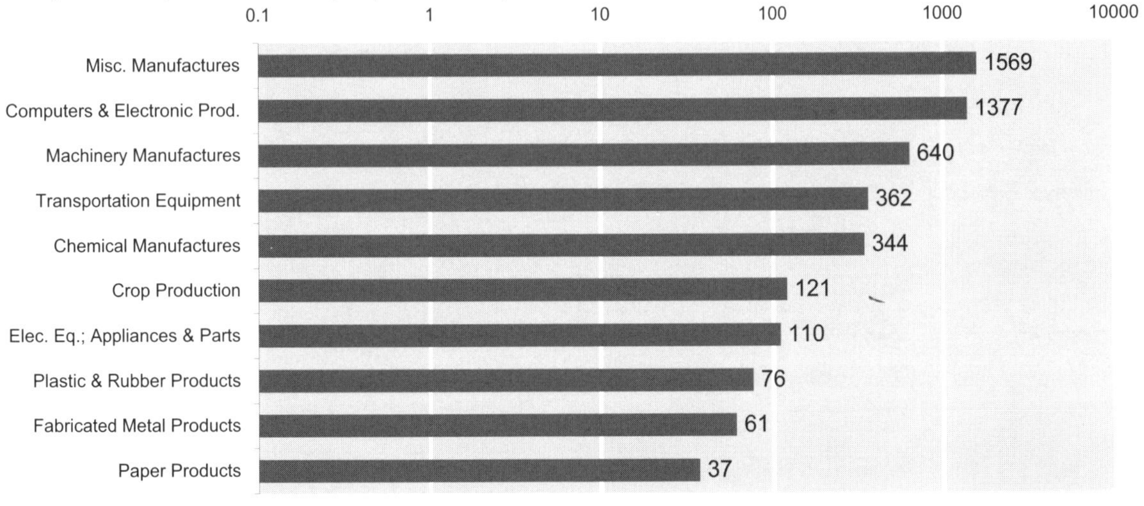

Source: Bureau of Economic Analysis; Office of Trade and Industry Information

Mississippi and Europe

Employment, Investment, and Trade Linkages

Employment

European investment in Mississippi supported 14,400 jobs in 2004; 37% of the jobs were in manufacturing.

Investment

Of the $6.8 billion invested in Mississippi in 2004, 53%, or $3.6 billion came from Europe.

Sources of FDI within Mississippi, 2004	
Country	**FDI ($ Millions)**
Canada	1,559
Japan	1,180
United Kingdom	1,005
Netherlands	776
Germany	593

Trade

In 2005, Europe purchased $784 million worth of goods from Mississippi. Chemicals and paper rank as the top exports to Europe.

Top European Export Markets, 2005	
Country	**Exports ($ Millions)**
Belgium	228
United Kingdom	197
Germany	92
Italy	58
Spain	56

Top Ten Exports to Europe ($ Millions)

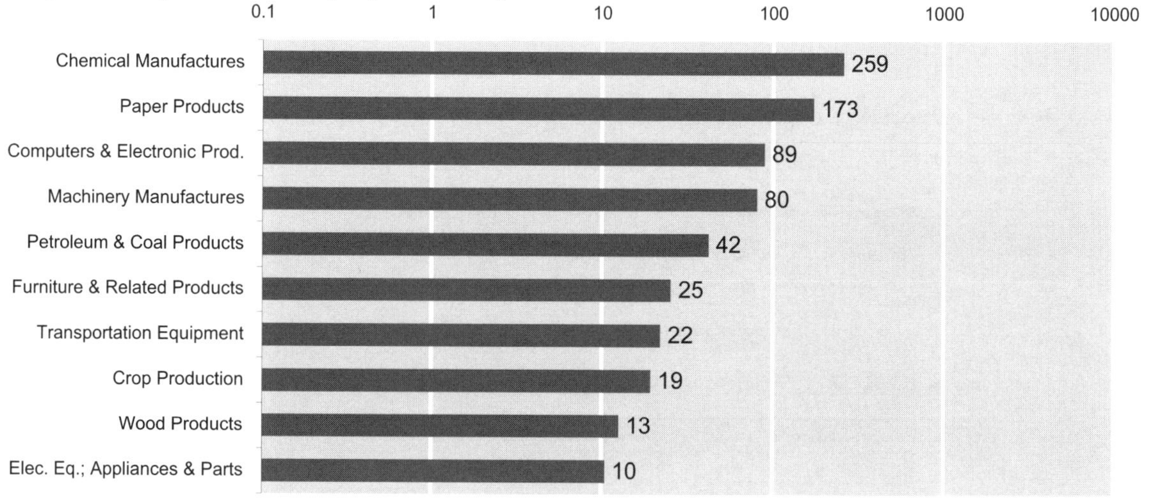

Source: Bureau of Economic Analysis; Office of Trade and Industry Information

Missouri and Europe

Employment, Investment, and Trade Linkages

Employment

European investment in Missouri supported 59,900 jobs in 2004; 44% of the jobs were in manufacturing.

Investment

Of the $16.0 billion invested in Missouri in 2004, 71%, or $11.3 billion came from Europe.

Sources of FDI within Missouri, 2004	
Country	**FDI ($ Millions)**
Germany	5,445
United Kingdom	1,642
France	1,381
Canada	1,380
Japan	1,126

Trade

In 2005, Europe purchased $1.8 billion worth of goods from Missouri.
Top exports included chemical products and machinery.

Top European Export Markets, 2005	
Country	**Exports ($ Millions)**
United Kingdom	375
Germany	311
Belgium	291
Italy	231
Netherlands	157

Top Ten Exports to Europe ($ Millions)

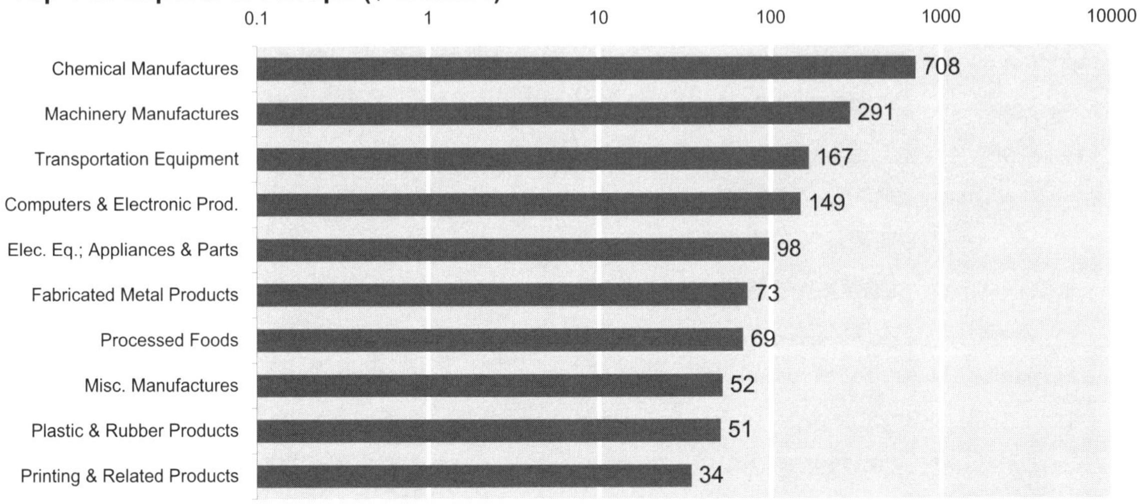

Source: Bureau of Economic Analysis; Office of Trade and Industry Information

Montana and Europe

Employment, Investment, and Trade Linkages

Employment

European investment in Montana supported 4,500 jobs in 2004; 7% of the jobs were in manufacturing.

Investment

Of the $2.2 billion invested in Montana in 2004, 64%, or $1.4 billion came from Europe.

Sources of FDI within Montana, 2004	
Country	**FDI ($ Millions)**
Canada	315
France	73
Germany	11
Netherlands	3
Italy	1

Trade

In 2005, Europe purchased $113 million worth of goods from Montana.
Exports are relatively small and skewed towards machinery and chemical goods.

Top European Export Markets, 2005	
Country	**Exports ($ Millions)**
Germany	49
United Kingdom	23
Netherlands	16
France	7
Finland	4

Top Ten Exports to Europe ($ Millions)

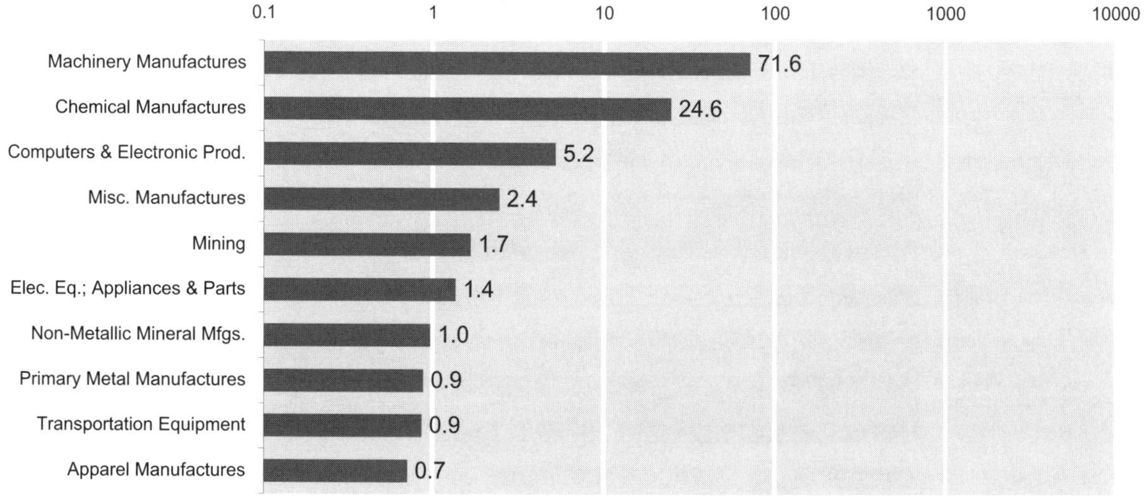

Source: Bureau of Economic Analysis; Office of Trade and Industry Information

Nebraska and Europe

Employment, Investment, and Trade Linkages

Employment

European investment in Nebraska supported 12,400 jobs in 2004; 31% of the jobs were in manufacturing.

Investment

Of the $2.0 billion invested in Nebraska in 2004, 45%, or $906 million came from Europe.

Sources of FDI within Nebraska, 2004	
Country	**FDI ($ Millions)**
Japan	437
Canada	315
Switzerland	235
Netherlands	157
Australia	153

Trade

In 2005, Europe purchased $417 million worth of goods from Nebraska.
Top exports from Nebraska are machinery and chemicals.

Top European Export Markets, 2005	
Country	**Exports ($ Millions)**
Netherlands	73
Germany	65
United Kingdom	63
France	50
Belgium	46

Top Ten Exports to Europe ($ Millions)

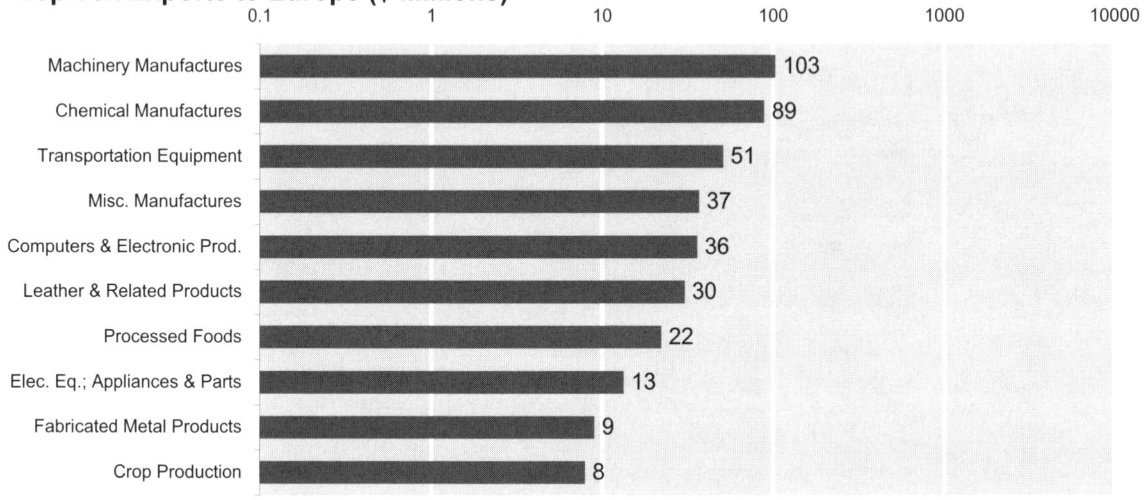

Source: Bureau of Economic Analysis; Office of Trade and Industry Information

Nevada and Europe

Employment, Investment, and Trade Linkages

Employment

European investment in Nevada supported 15,600 jobs in 2004; 11% of the jobs were in manufacturing.

Investment

Of the $6.5 billion invested in Nevada in 2004, 25%, or $1.6 billion came from Europe.

Sources of FDI within Nevada, 2004	
Country	**FDI ($ Millions)**
Canada	3,636
United Kingdom	858
Japan	502
Australia	240
Netherlands	228

Trade

In 2005, Europe purchased $434 million worth of goods from Nevada.
Manufactured goods, as well as computers and electronics, are the top exports to the EU.

Top European Export Markets, 2005	
Country	**Exports ($ Millions)**
Switzerland	1,833
Netherlands	104
United Kingdom	78
Belgium	52
France	49

Top Ten Exports to Europe ($ Millions)

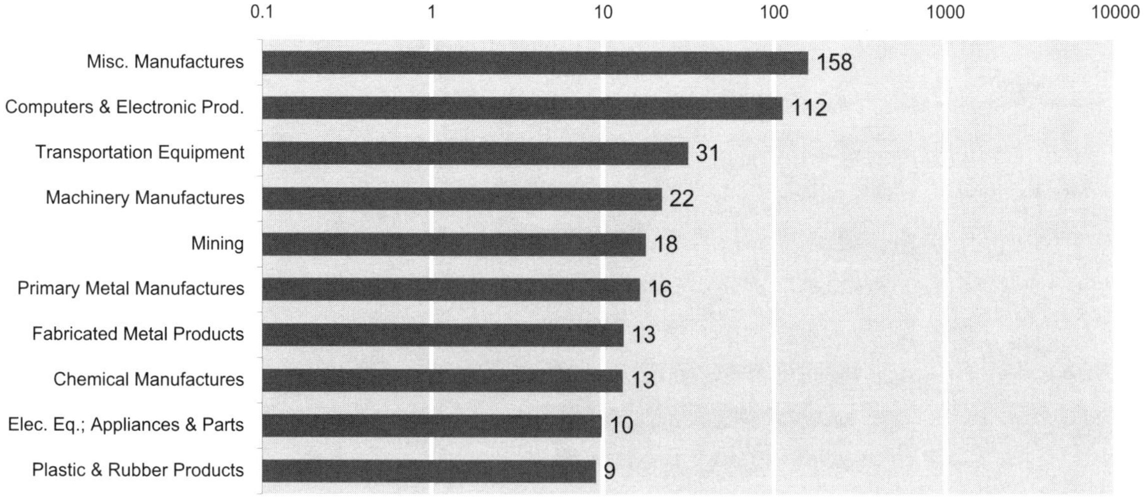

Source: Bureau of Economic Analysis; Office of Trade and Industry Information

New Hampshire and Europe

Employment, Investment, and Trade Linkages

Employment

European investment in New Hampshire supported 32,300 jobs in 2004; 43% of the jobs were in manufacturing.

Investment

Of the $4.7 billion invested in New Hampshire in 2004, 77%, or $3.6 billion came from Europe.

Sources of FDI within New Hampshire, 2004	
Country	**FDI ($ Millions)**
United Kingdom	1,429
Germany	800
Japan	378
France	366
Canada	357

Trade

In 2005, Europe purchased $858 million worth of goods from New Hampshire. Computers, electronic products and machinery are the top exports to Europe.

Top European Export Markets, 2005	
Country	**Exports ($ Millions)**
Netherlands	216
United Kingdom	176
Germany	151
France	74
Italy	71

Top Ten Exports to Europe ($ Millions)

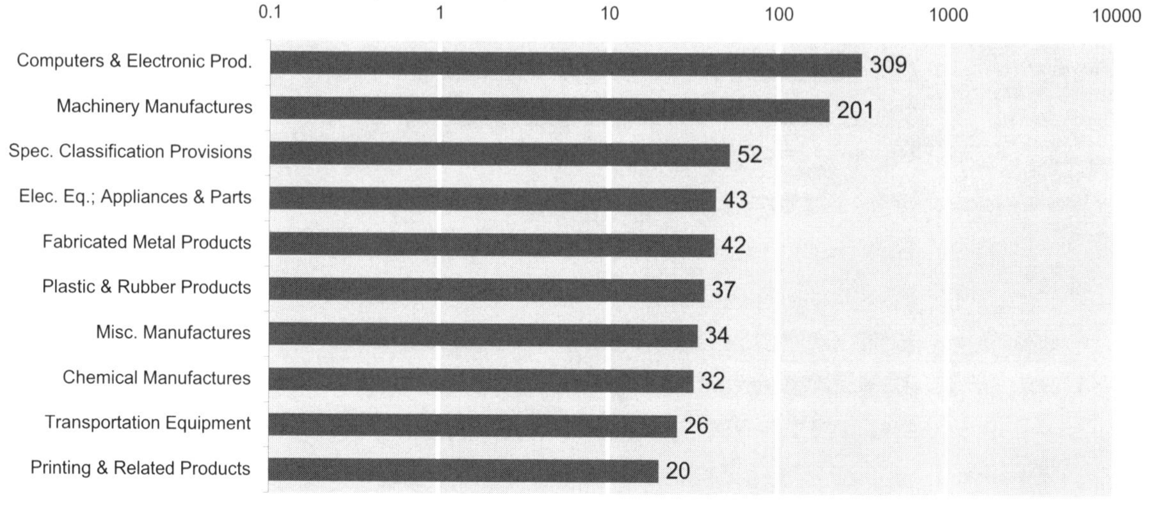

Source: Bureau of Economic Analysis; Office of Trade and Industry Information

New Jersey and Europe

Employment, Investment, and Trade Linkages

Employment

European investment in New Jersey supported 170,300 jobs in 2004; 24% of the jobs were in manufacturing.

Investment

Of the $33.8 billion invested in New Jersey in 2004, 74%, or $25.0 billion came from Europe.

Sources of FDI within New Jersey, 2004	
Country	**FDI ($ Millions)**
Germany	8,554
Switzerland	4,346
Japan	3,966
United Kingdom	3,798
France	3,511

Trade

In 2005, Europe purchased $6.8 billion worth of goods from New Jersey.
Exports consist of high-end goods, like chemicals (pharmaceuticals) and computers.

Top European Export Markets, 2005	
Country	**Exports ($ Millions)**
United Kingdom	1,766
Germany	1,294
France	817
Italy	795
Netherlands	588

Top Ten Exports to Europe ($ Millions)

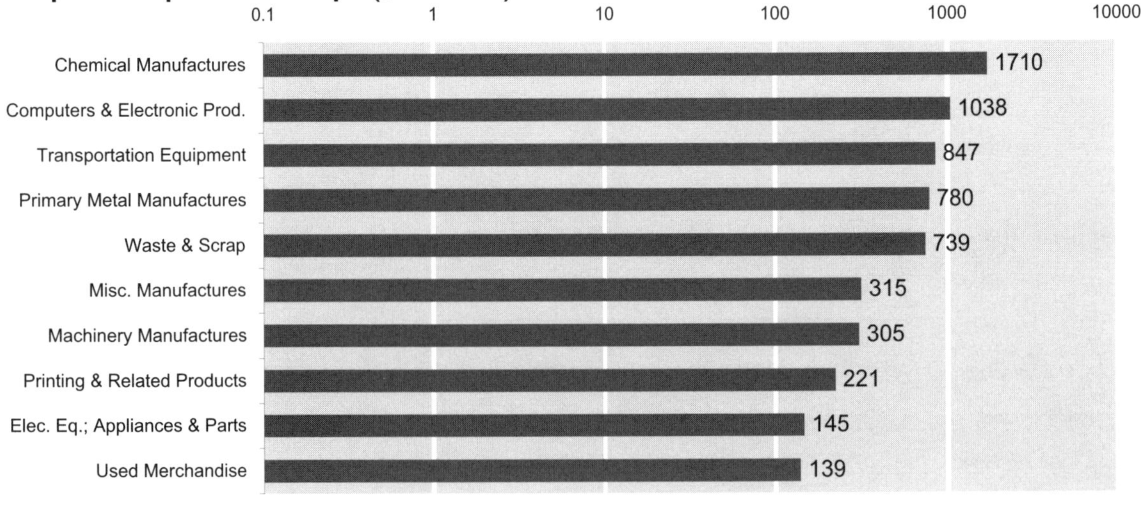

Source: Bureau of Economic Analysis; Office of Trade and Industry Information

New Mexico and Europe

Employment, Investment, and Trade Linkages

Employment

European investment in New Mexico supported 7,800 jobs in 2004; 17% of the jobs were in manufacturing.

Investment

Of the $3.8 billion invested in New Mexico in 2004, 76%, or $2.9 billion came from Europe.

Sources of FDI within New Mexico, 2004

Country	FDI ($ Millions)
Germany	213
France	153
Japan	142
Sweden	33
Canada	31

Trade

In 2005, Europe purchased $262 million worth of goods from New Mexico. Exports are relatively small and are skewed toward computers and related goods.

Top European Export Markets, 2005

Country	Exports ($ Millions)
Ireland	75
United Kingdom	47
Germany	42
Belgium	36
France	21

Top Ten Exports to Europe ($ Millions)

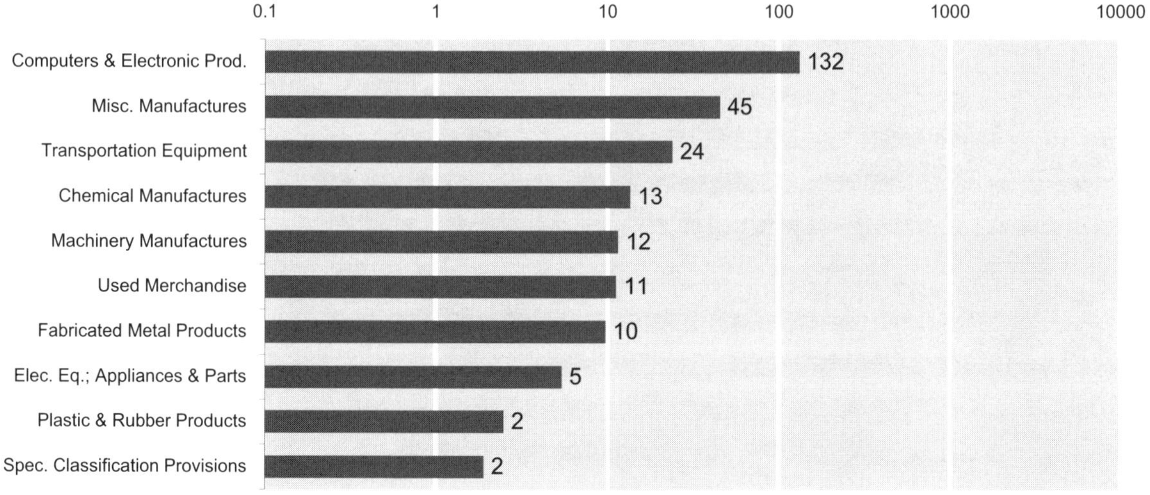

Source: Bureau of Economic Analysis; Office of Trade and Industry Information

New York and Europe

Employment, Investment, and Trade Linkages

Employment

European investment in New York supported 289,400 jobs in 2004; 11% of the jobs were in manufacturing.

Investment

Of the $60.6 billion invested in New York in 2004, 65%, or $39.1 billion came from Europe.

Sources of FDI within New York, 2004	
Country	**FDI ($ Millions)**
United Kingdom	12,339
Germany	8,971
Canada	8,551
France	7,453
Japan	6,695

Trade

In 2005, Europe purchased $12.9 billion worth of goods from New York. Exports run the gamut -- from computers to plastics.

Top European Export Markets, 2005	
Country	**Exports ($ Millions)**
United Kingdom	2,894
Germany	2,222
Switzerland	2,214
Belgium	2,024
France	1,407

Top Ten Exports to Europe ($ Millions)

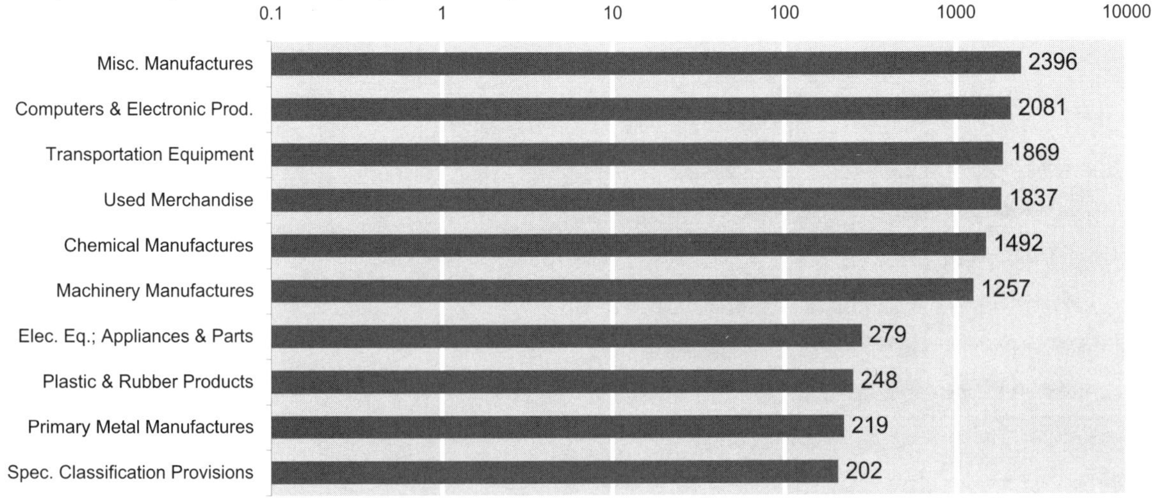

Source: Bureau of Economic Analysis; Office of Trade and Industry Information

North Carolina and Europe

Employment, Investment, and Trade Linkages

Employment

European investment in North Carolina supported 158,200 jobs in 2004; 33% of the jobs were in manufacturing.

Investment

Of the $23.9 billion invested in North Carolina in 2004, 69%, or $16.6 billion came from Europe.

Sources of FDI within North Carolina, 2004	
Country	**FDI ($ Millions)**
United Kingdom	5,242
Germany	4,483
Japan	2,805
Canada	2,231
Netherlands	1,475

Trade

In 2005, Europe purchased $4.3 billion worth of goods from North Carolina. Exports include such high-tech goods as chemicals, computers and machinery.

Top European Export Markets, 2005	
Country	**Exports ($ Millions)**
United Kingdom	931
Germany	685
France	604
Italy	556
Netherlands	393

Top Ten Exports to Europe ($ Millions)

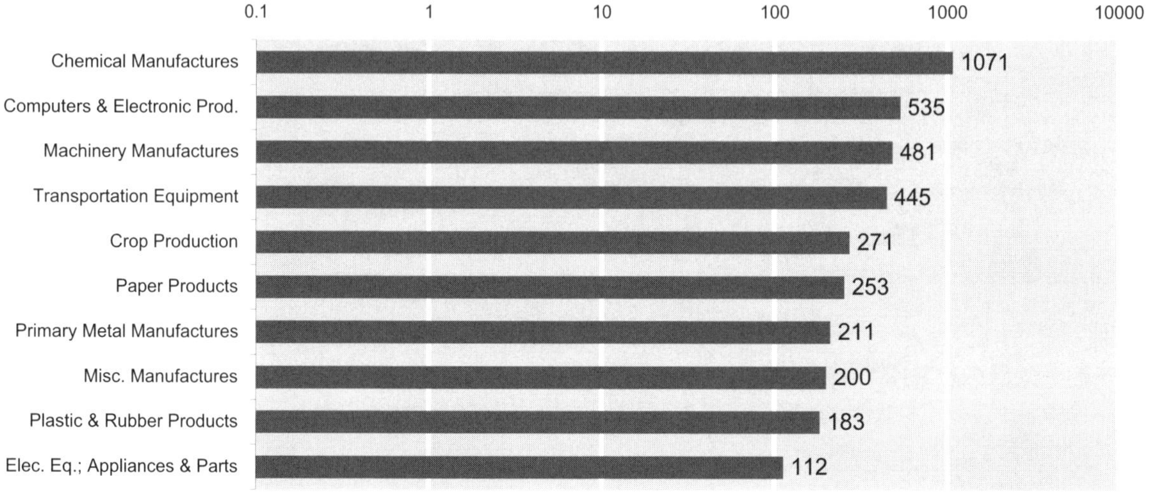

Source: Bureau of Economic Analysis; Office of Trade and Industry Information

North Dakota and Europe

Employment, Investment, and Trade Linkages

Employment

European investment in North Dakota supported over 3,000 jobs in 2004.

Investment

Of the $1.4 billion invested in North Dakota in 2004, roughly 15% came from the UK, Germany and the Netherlands.

Sources of FDI within North Dakota, 2004	
Country	**FDI ($ Millions)**
Canada	407
United Kingdom	84
Germany	73
Netherlands	49
Australia	6

Trade

In 2005, Europe purchased $287 million worth of goods from North Dakota.
By a large percentage, the state's top export consists of machinery.

Top European Export Markets, 2005	
Country	**Exports ($ Millions)**
Belgium	109
Italy	45
United Kingdom	25
Spain	25
Netherlands	23

Top Ten Exports to Europe ($ Millions)

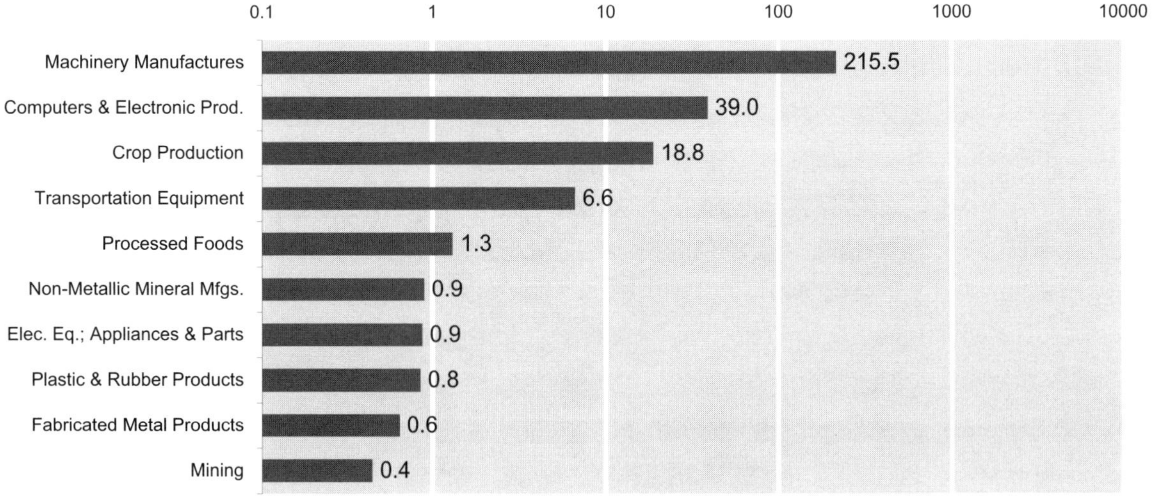

Source: Bureau of Economic Analysis; Office of Trade and Industry Information

Ohio and Europe

Employment, Investment, and Trade Linkages

Employment

European investment in Ohio supported 128,900 jobs in 2004; 40% of the jobs were in manufacturing.

Investment

Of the $32.9 billion invested in Ohio in 2004, 56%, or $18.5 billion came from Europe.

Sources of FDI within Ohio, 2004	
Country	**FDI ($ Millions)**
Japan	10,414
Germany	7,874
United Kingdom	5,547
Canada	1,902
France	1,718

Trade

In 2005, Europe purchased $5.7 billion worth of goods from Ohio.
Transportation equipment, machinery and chemicals are the state's top exports to Europe.

Top European Export Markets, 2005	
Country	**Exports ($ Millions)**
United Kingdom	1,154
Germany	1,108
France	954
Netherlands	610
Belgium	523

Top Ten Exports to Europe ($ Millions)

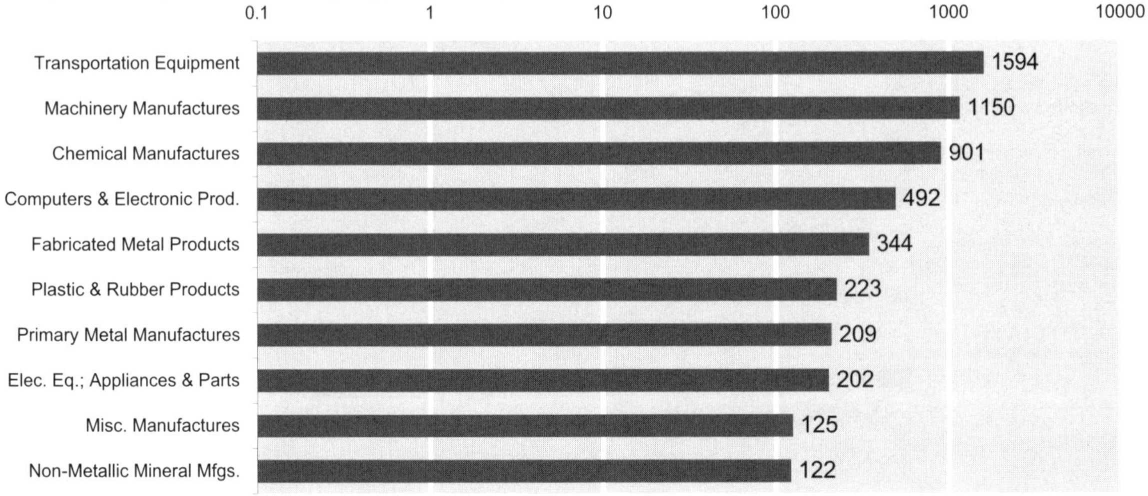

Source: Bureau of Economic Analysis; Office of Trade and Industry Information

Oklahoma and Europe

Employment, Investment, and Trade Linkages

Employment

European investment in Oklahoma supported 20,200 jobs in 2004; 35% of the jobs were in manufacturing.

Investment

Of the $8.2 billion invested in Oklahoma in 2004, 71%, or $5.8 billion came from Europe.

Sources of FDI within Oklahoma, 2004	
Country	**FDI ($ Millions)**
United Kingdom	2,366
Netherlands	1,568
France	780
Japan	534
Canada	268

Trade

In 2005, Europe purchased $453 million worth of goods from Oklahoma.
Top exports include machinery, transportation equipment and computers.

Top European Export Markets, 2005	
Country	**Exports ($ Millions)**
Germany	93
United Kingdom	87
Belgium	76
Netherlands	62
France	44

Top Ten Exports to Europe ($ Millions)

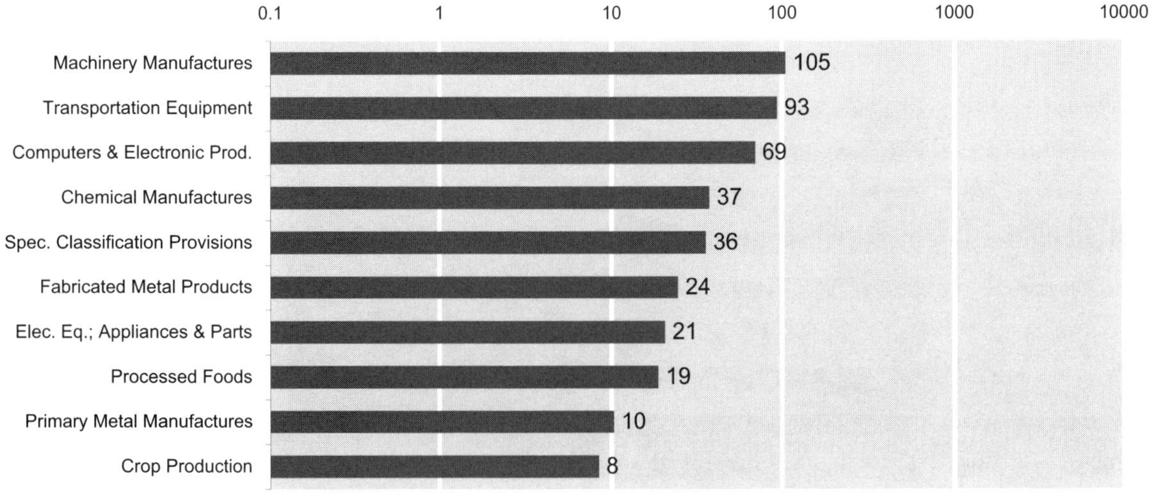

Source: Bureau of Economic Analysis; Office of Trade and Industry Information

Oregon and Europe

Employment, Investment, and Trade Linkages

Employment

European investment in Oregon supported 32,600 jobs in 2004; 16% of the jobs were in manufacturing.

Investment

Of the $11.7 billion invested in Oregon in 2004, 50%, or $5.9 billion came from Europe.

Sources of FDI within Oregon, 2004

Country	FDI ($ Millions)
United Kingdom	3,653
Canada	1,924
Japan	1,654
Germany	1,547
France	183

Trade

In 2005, Europe purchased $1.6 billion worth of goods from Oregon.
Roughly 40% of Oregon's exports to Europe consist of computers and related products.

Top European Export Markets, 2005

Country	Exports ($ Millions)
Germany	320
France	223
United Kingdom	221
Netherlands	173
Italy	115

Top Ten Exports to Europe ($ Millions)

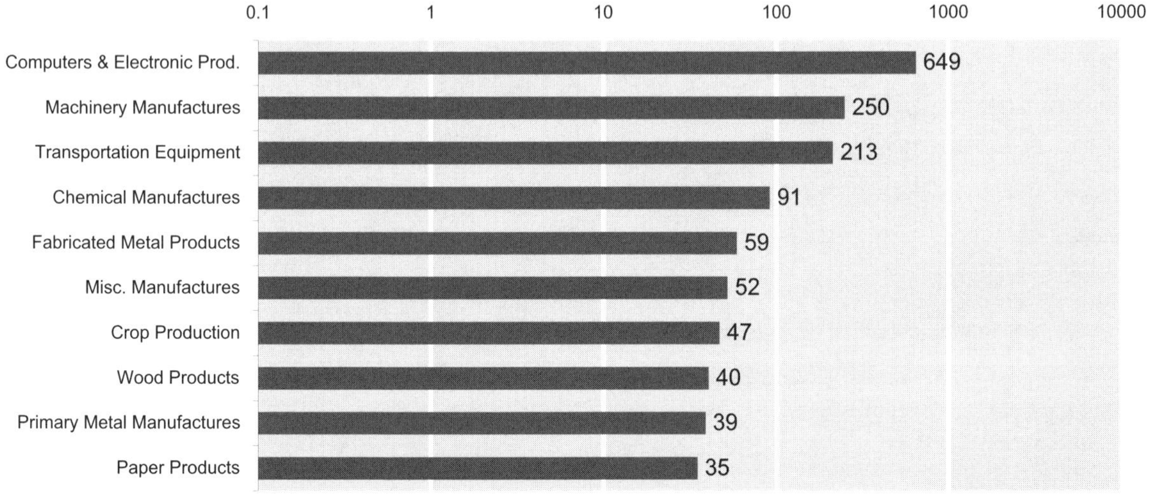

Source: Bureau of Economic Analysis; Office of Trade and Industry Information

Pennsylvania and Europe

Employment, Investment, and Trade Linkages

Employment

European investment in Pennsylvania supported 173,200 jobs in 2004; 31% of the jobs were in manufacturing.

Investment

Of the $30.2 billion invested in Pennsylvania in 2004, 74%, or $22.3 billion came from Europe.

Sources of FDI within Pennsylvania, 2004	
Country	**FDI ($ Millions)**
Germany	6,657
United Kingdom	6,528
France	3,165
Canada	2,746
Netherlands	1,999

Trade

In 2005, Europe purchased $5.3 billion worth of goods from Pennsylvania.
Exports are relatively diverse, ranging from chemicals to transportation equipment.

Top European Export Markets, 2005	
Country	**Exports ($ Millions)**
United Kingdom	1,029
Germany	913
Belgium	813
Netherlands	622
France	447

Top Ten Exports to Europe ($ Millions)

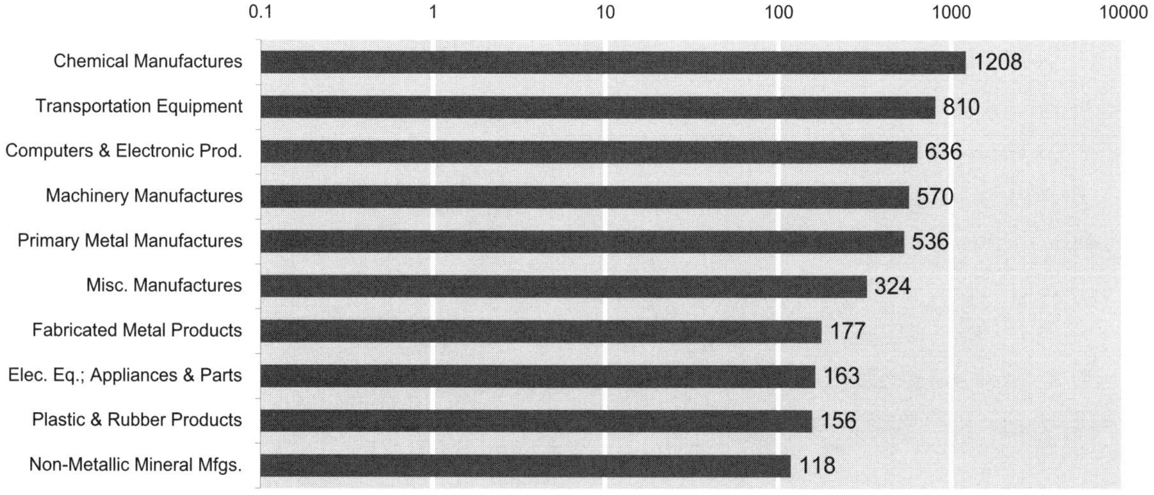

Source: Bureau of Economic Analysis; Office of Trade and Industry Information

Rhode Island and Europe

Employment, Investment, and Trade Linkages

Employment

European investment in Rhode Island supported 22,200 jobs in 2004; 9% of the jobs were in manufacturing.

Investment

Of the $3.4 billion invested in Rhode Island in 2004, 76%, or $2.6 billion came from Europe.

Sources of FDI within Rhode Island, 2004	
Country	**FDI ($ Millions)**
United Kingdom	1,636
Germany	349
Canada	176
France	103
Switzerland	78

Trade

In 2005, Europe purchased $312 million worth of goods from Rhode Island. Manufactured goods and electronic products make up the bulk of exports.

Top European Export Markets, 2005	
Country	**Exports ($ Millions)**
United Kingdom	65
Germany	54
Belgium	32
Italy	31
France	25

Top Ten Exports to Europe ($ Millions)

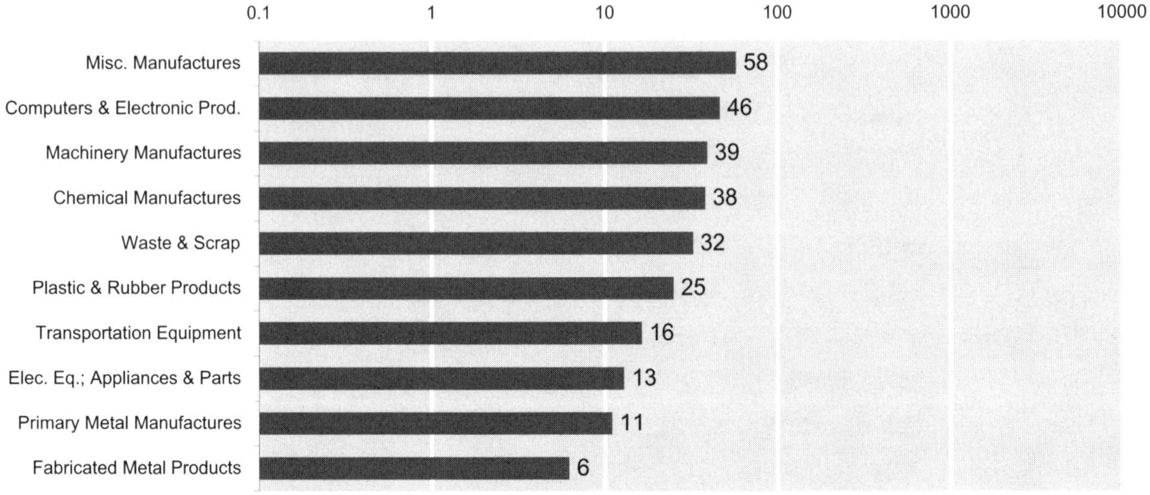

Source: Bureau of Economic Analysis; Office of Trade and Industry Information

South Carolina and Europe

Employment, Investment, and Trade Linkages

Employment

European investment in South Carolina supported 94,900 jobs in 2004; 46% of the jobs were in manufacturing.

Investment

Of the $21.8 billion invested in South Carolina in 2004, 73%, or $15.9 billion came from Europe.

Sources of FDI within South Carolina, 2004

Country	FDI ($ Millions)
Germany	4,286
Japan	3,438
France	3,334
United Kingdom	2,619
Switzerland	1,644

Trade

In 2005, Europe purchased $5.2 billion worth of goods from South Carolina. Roughly half of the state's exports consist of transportation equipment.

Top European Export Markets, 2005

Country	Exports ($ Millions)
Germany	2,357
United Kingdom	971
Netherlands	467
Belgium	426
France	348

Top Ten Exports to Europe ($ Millions)

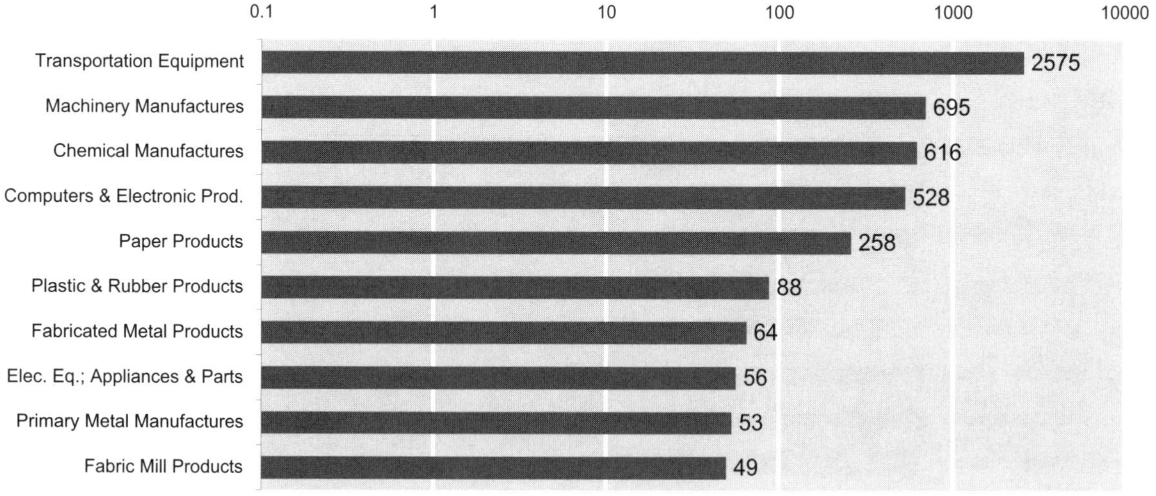

Source: Bureau of Economic Analysis; Office of Trade and Industry Information

South Dakota and Europe

Employment, Investment, and Trade Linkages

Employment

European investment in South Dakota supported 2,700 jobs in 2004; 41% of the jobs were in manufacturing.

Investment

Of the $750 million invested in South Dakota in 2004, 46%, or $348 million came from Europe.

Sources of FDI within South Dakota, 2004	
Country	**FDI ($ Millions)**
United Kingdom	247
Canada	122
Japan	46
Sweden	28
Germany	15

Trade

In 2005, Europe purchased $131 million worth of goods from South Dakota. Computers and machinery are the state's top export to Europe.

Top European Export Markets, 2005	
Country	**Exports ($ Millions)**
Germany	39
United Kingdom	30
Italy	17
France	13
Netherlands	5

Top Ten Exports to Europe ($ Millions)

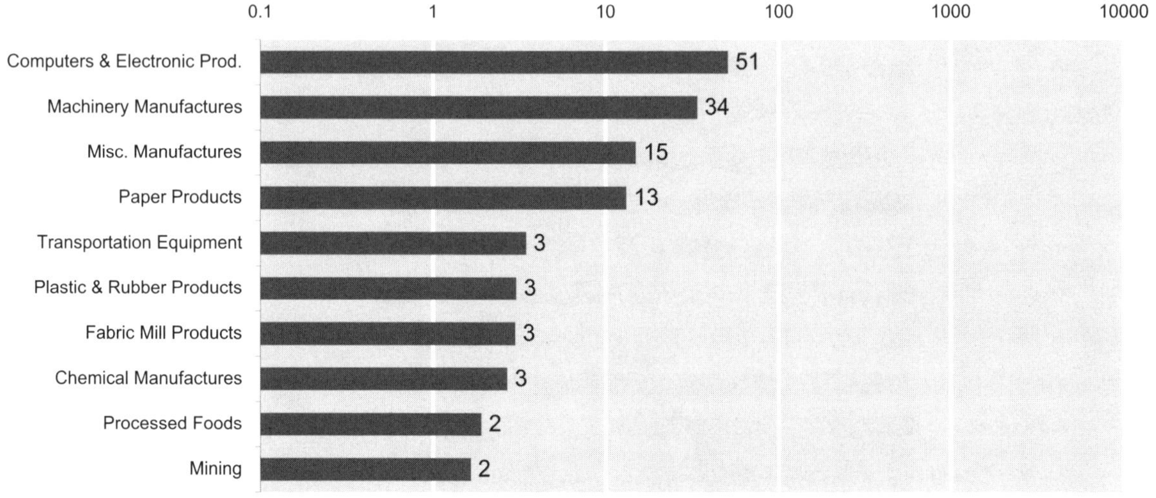

Source: Bureau of Economic Analysis; Office of Trade and Industry Information

Tennessee and Europe

Employment, Investment, and Trade Linkages

Employment

European investment in Tennessee supported 70,800 jobs in 2004; 36% of the jobs were in manufacturing.

Investment

Of the $19.9 billion invested in Tennessee in 2004, 43%, or $8.5 billion came from Europe.

Sources of FDI within Tennessee, 2004	
Country	**FDI ($ Millions)**
Japan	8,130
United Kingdom	2,285
Germany	2,231
Canada	1,934
France	1,247

Trade

In 2005, Europe purchased $3.7 billion worth of goods from Tennessee. Manufactured goods, ranging from transportation equipment to chemicals to computers, make up the bulk of exports.

Top European Export Markets, 2005	
Country	**Exports ($ Millions)**
United Kingdom	738
Germany	677
Netherlands	635
Belgium	378
France	307

Top Ten Exports to Europe ($ Millions)

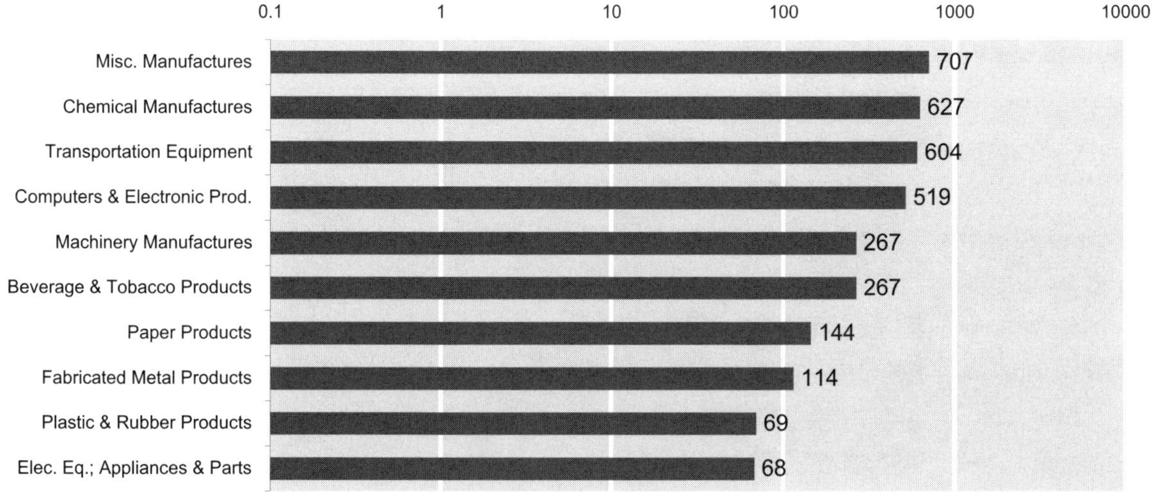

Source: Bureau of Economic Analysis; Office of Trade and Industry Information

Texas and Europe

Employment, Investment, and Trade Linkages

Employment

European investment in Texas supported 228,500 jobs in 2004; 24% of the jobs were in manufacturing.

Investment

Of the $83.7 billion invested in Texas in 2004, 66%, or $55.3 billion came from Europe.

Sources of FDI within Texas, 2004	
Country	**FDI ($ Millions)**
United Kingdom	17,486
Germany	11,955
Netherlands	8,678
France	7,350
Japan	6,526

Trade

In 2005, Europe purchased $13.0 billion worth of goods from Texas.
Top exports include chemicals, computers and machinery.

Top European Export Markets, 2005	
Country	**Exports ($ Millions)**
Netherlands	2,653
United Kingdom	2,523
Belgium	2,177
Germany	1,716
France	1,267

Top Ten Exports to Europe ($ Millions)

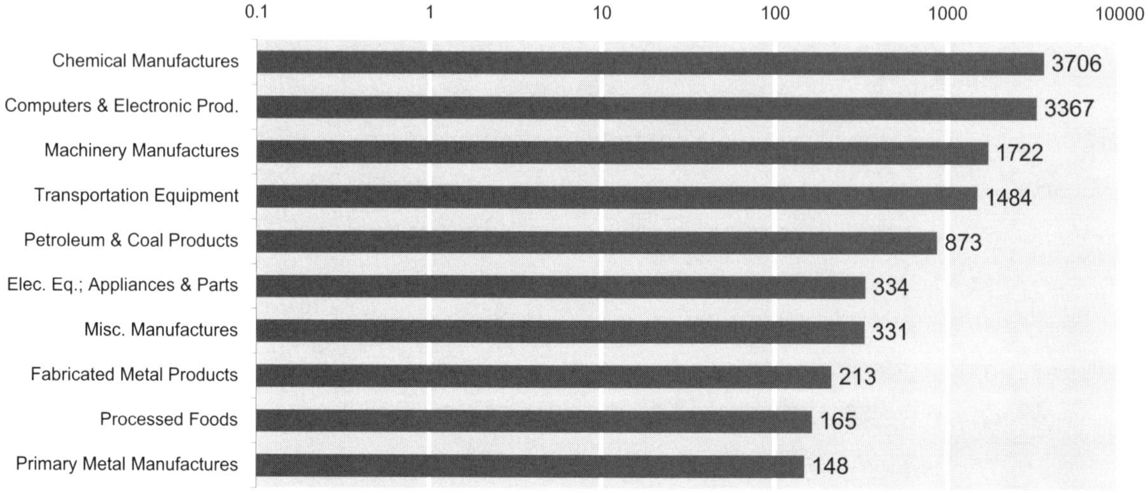

Source: Bureau of Economic Analysis; Office of Trade and Industry Information

Utah and Europe

Employment, Investment, and Trade Linkages

Employment

European investment in Utah supported 24,800 jobs in 2004; 26% of the jobs were in manufacturing.

Investment

Of the $11.4 billion invested in Utah in 2004, 91%, or $10.4 billion came from Europe.

Sources of FDI within Utah, 2004	
Country	**FDI ($ Millions)**
Switzerland	421
Canada	330
Germany	309
Japan	185
Netherlands	106

Trade

In 2005, Europe purchased $2.1 billion worth of goods from Utah.
Primary metals dominate exports to Europe.

Top European Export Markets, 2005	
Country	**Exports ($ Millions)**
United Kingdom	1,105
Switzerland	777
Belgium	428
Germany	208
Netherlands	119

Top Ten Exports to Europe ($ Millions)

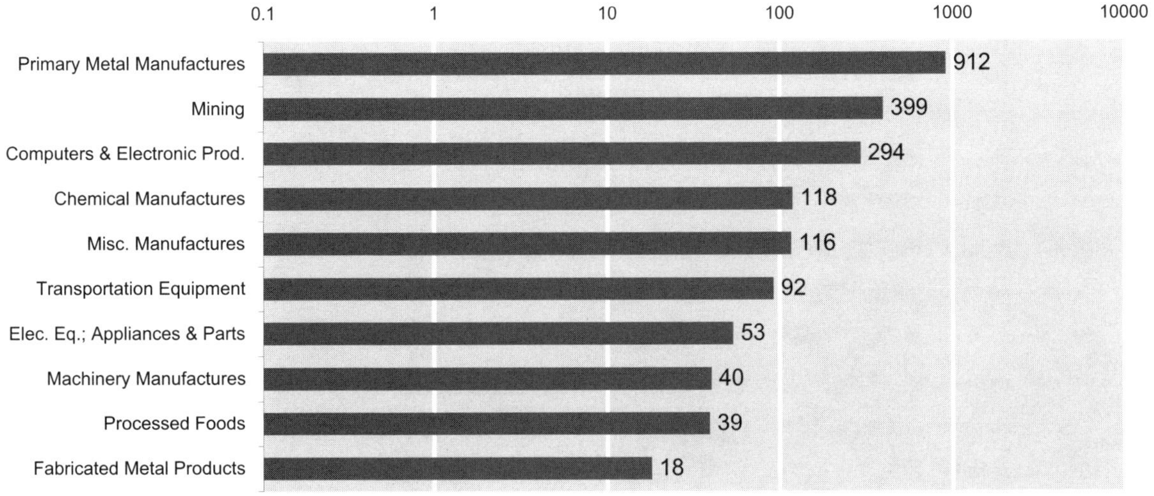

Source: Bureau of Economic Analysis; Office of Trade and Industry Information

Vermont and Europe

Employment, Investment, and Trade Linkages

Employment

European investment in Vermont supported 8,800 jobs in 2004; 18% of the jobs were in manufacturing.

Investment

Of the $1.4 billion invested in Vermont in 2004, 79%, or $1.1 billion came from Europe.

Sources of FDI within Vermont, 2004

Country	FDI ($ Millions)
Canada	227
United Kingdom	151
France	71
Germany	64
Japan	39

Trade

In 2005, Europe purchased $390 million worth of goods from Vermont.
By a wide margin, computers are the top export to Europe.

Top European Export Markets, 2005

Country	Exports ($ Millions)
Ireland	140
United Kingdom	81
Germany	34
Czech Republic	26
Netherlands	26

Top Ten Exports to Europe ($ Millions)

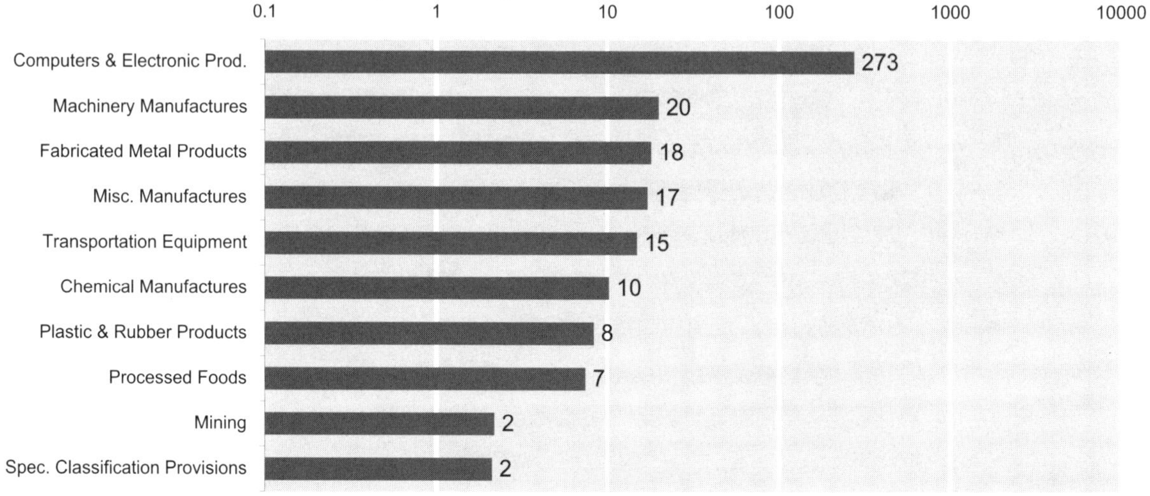

Source: Bureau of Economic Analysis; Office of Trade and Industry Information

Virginia and Europe
Employment, Investment, and Trade Linkages

Employment
European investment in Virginia supported 99,000 jobs in 2004; 25% of the jobs were in manufacturing.

Investment
Of the $16.4 billion invested in Virginia in 2004, 75%, or $12.3 billion came from Europe.

Sources of FDI within Virginia, 2004

Country	FDI ($ Millions)
Germany	4,682
Japan	2,018
Netherlands	1,682
United Kingdom	1,296
France	1,146

Trade
In 2005, Europe purchased $4.0 billion worth of goods from Virginia.
Top exports include computers, transportation equipment and chemicals.

Top European Export Markets, 2005

Country	Exports ($ Millions)
Germany	1,179
United Kingdom	744
Belgium	417
Netherlands	410
France	279

Top Ten Exports to Europe ($ Millions)

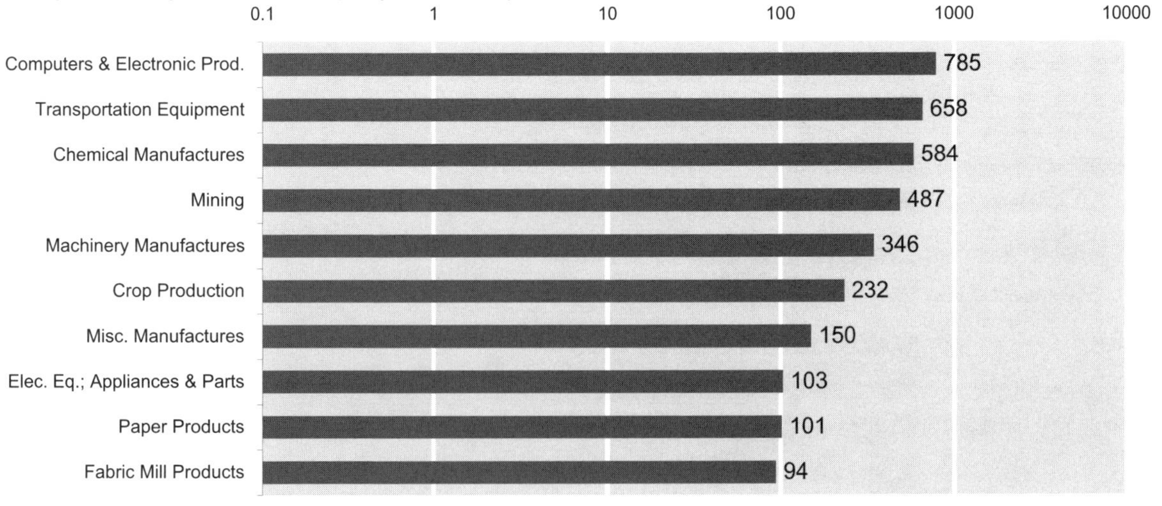

Source: Bureau of Economic Analysis; Office of Trade and Industry Information

Washington and Europe

Employment, Investment, and Trade Linkages

Employment

European investment in Washington supported 48,800 jobs in 2004; 23% of the jobs were in manufacturing.

Investment

Of the $17.5 billion invested in Washington in 2004, 52%, or $9.1 billion came from Europe.

Sources of FDI within Washington, 2004	
Country	**FDI ($ Millions)**
United Kingdom	2,935
Japan	2,816
Germany	2,789
Canada	2,682
Netherlands	1,388

Trade

In 2005, Europe purchased $6.4 billion worth of goods from Washington. Transportation equipment dominates exports to Europe.

Top European Export Markets, 2005	
Country	**Exports ($ Millions)**
Ireland	1,846
France	978
United Kingdom	887
Netherlands	649
Germany	552

Top Ten Exports to Europe ($ Millions)

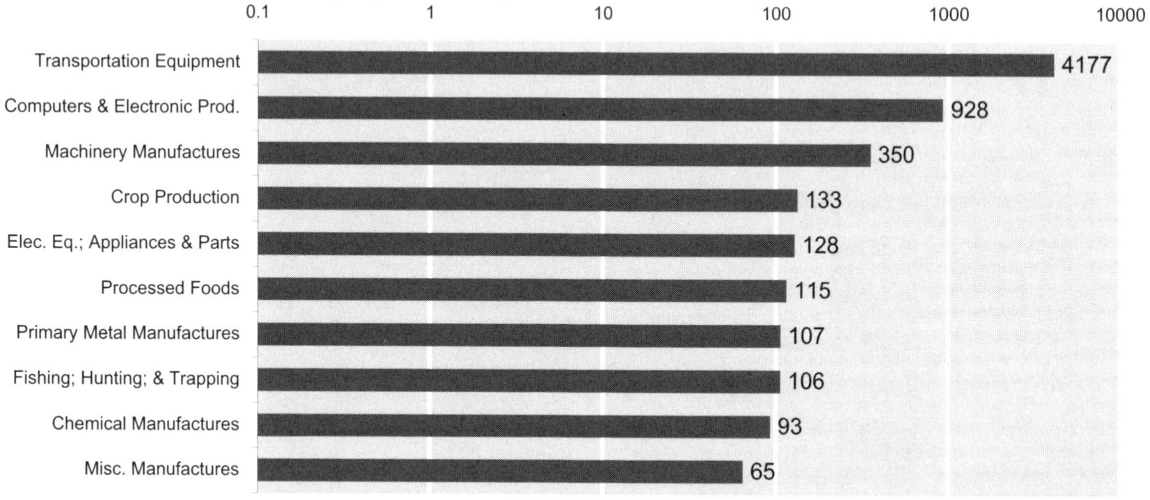

Source: Bureau of Economic Analysis; Office of Trade and Industry Information

West Virginia and Europe

Employment, Investment, and Trade Linkages

Employment

European investment in West Virginia supported 13,000 jobs in 2004; 47% of the jobs were in manufacturing.

Investment

Of the $5.7 billion invested in West Virginia in 2004, 65%, or $3.7 billion came from Europe.

Sources of FDI within West Virginia, 2004

Country	FDI ($ Millions)
Germany	1,893
Japan	1,202
Canada	627
United Kingdom	506
France	474

Trade

In 2005, Europe purchased $738 million worth of goods from West Virginia. Chemical products are the state's top export to Europe.

Top European Export Markets, 2005

Country	Exports ($ Millions)
Belgium	288
Netherlands	140
Italy	92
United Kingdom	83
France	61

Top Ten Exports to Europe ($ Millions)

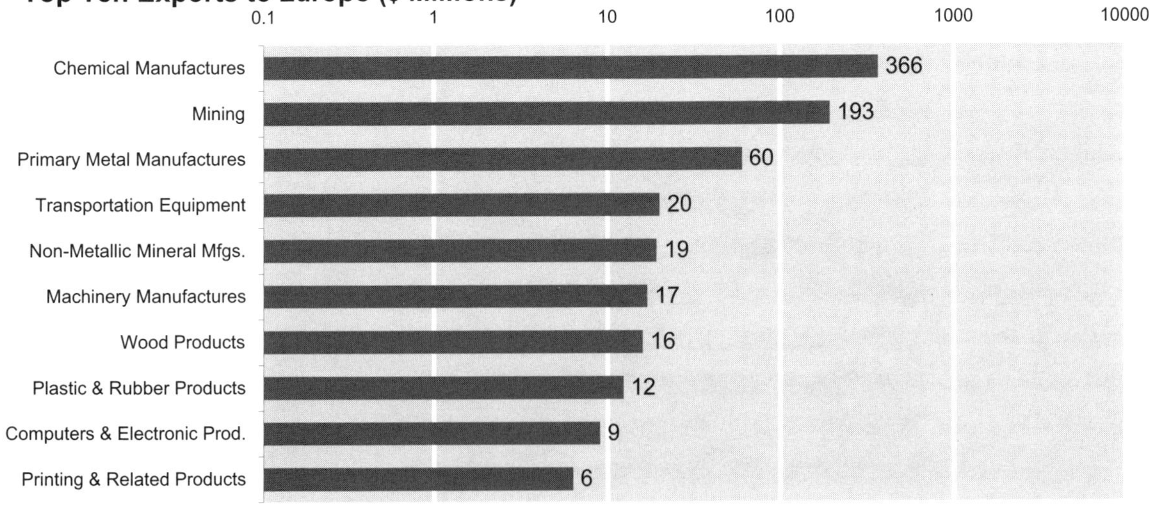

Source: Bureau of Economic Analysis; Office of Trade and Industry Information

Wisconsin and Europe

Employment, Investment, and Trade Linkages

Employment

European investment in Wisconsin supported 63,600 jobs in 2004; 46% of the jobs were in manufacturing.

Investment

Of the $15.9 billion invested in Wisconsin in 2004, 74%, or $11.7 billion came from Europe.

Sources of FDI within Wisconsin, 2004	
Country	**FDI ($ Millions)**
Canada	3,195
Germany	2,982
United Kingdom	1,040
France	938
Switzerland	511

Trade

In 2005, Europe purchased $3.2 billion worth of goods from Wisconsin.
Computers and machinery are the top exports to Europe.

Top European Export Markets, 2005	
Country	**Exports ($ Millions)**
United Kingdom	643
Germany	550
France	415
Belgium	376
Italy	305

Top Ten Exports to Europe ($ Millions)

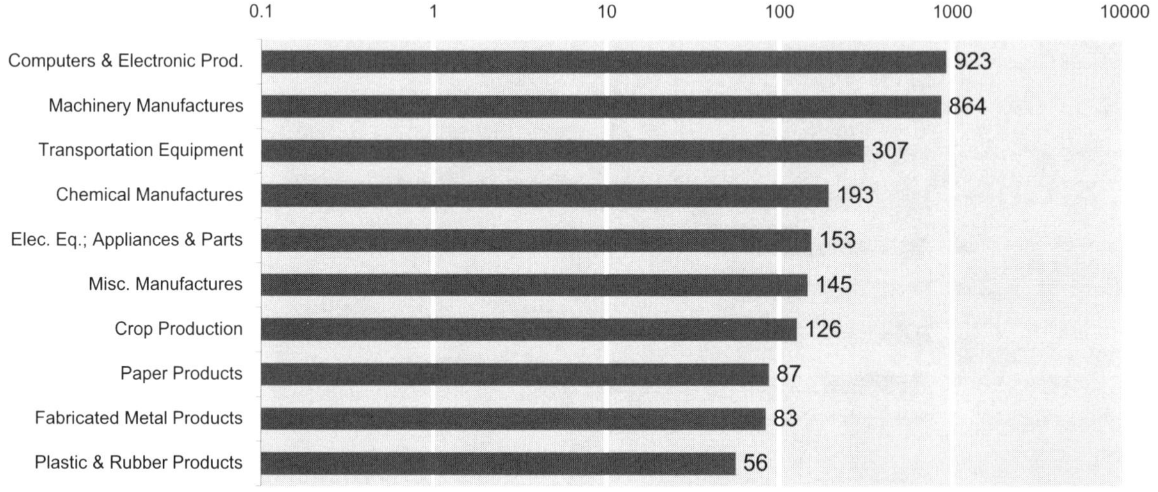

Source: Bureau of Economic Analysis; Office of Trade and Industry Information

Wyoming and Europe

Employment, Investment, and Trade Linkages

Employment

European investment in Wyoming supported 6,100 jobs in 2004; 13% of the jobs were in manufacturing.

Investment

Of the $12.4 billion invested in Wyoming in 2004, 70%, or $8.7 billion came from Europe.

Sources of FDI within Wyoming, 2004	
Country	**FDI ($ Millions)**
United Kingdom	6,881
France	59
Germany	35
Japan	32
Sweden	12

Trade

In 2005, Europe purchased $63 million worth of goods from Wyoming.
By a wide margin, chemicals are the top export to Europe.

Top European Export Markets, 2005	
Country	**Exports ($ Millions)**
Belgium	14
Spain	14
United Kingdom	12
Netherlands	11
France	5

Top Ten Exports to Europe ($ Millions)

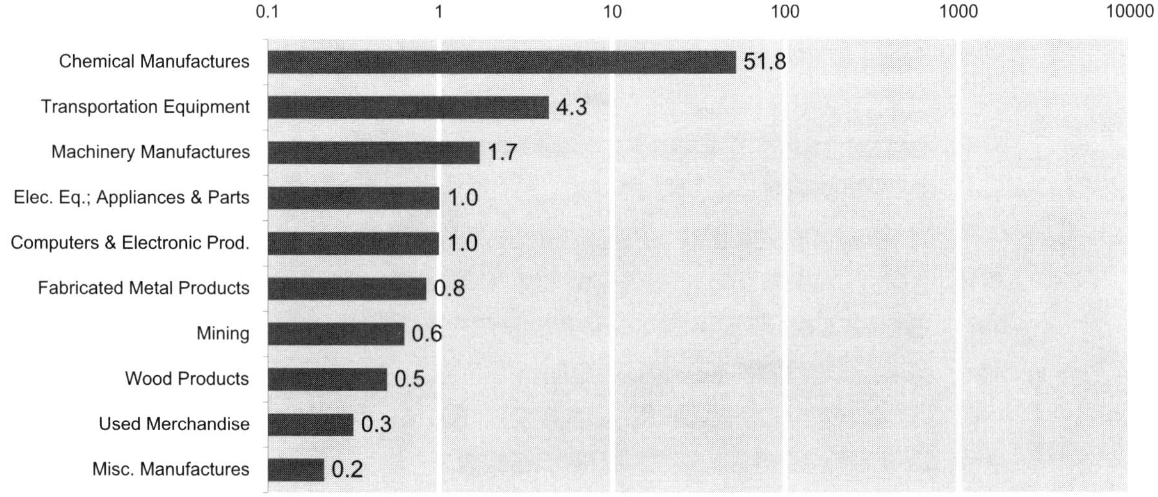

Source: Bureau of Economic Analysis; Office of Trade and Industry Information

Chapter 4
U.S. Commerce and Europe: A Country-by-Country Comparison

2005 was an unusual year for U.S. investment flows to the world, due to the American Jobs Creation Act of 2004. This legislation offered a one-time incentive to U.S. multinationals to repatriate earnings back to the United States. For a variety of reasons, many American firms did just that, repatriating billions of dollars based on this one-off opportunity. The effect was to sharply reduce reinvested earnings—one of three key components of foreign direct investment—thereby dramatically lowering aggregate U.S. foreign direct investment outflows for the year to the rest of the world.

Indeed, in 2005 there was a net outflow of U.S. FDI from Europe of $37.5 billion, in contrast to a net inflow of $93 billion in 2004.

In 2006, however, strong U.S. FDI flows to Europe quickly resumed their normal pattern, totaling $51 billion in the first half of the year alone, up 53% from the same period in 2005. Europe accounted for 47% of total US FDI in the first half of 2006.

U.S. Foreign Direct Investment Outflows[1]

Cumulative totals, 2000 - 2005, $ billions

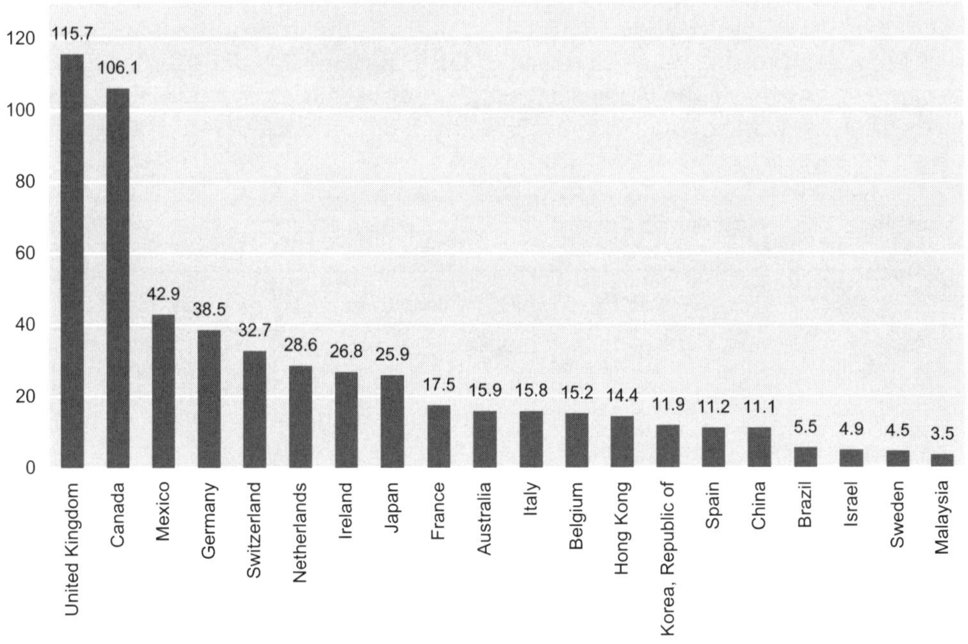

Source: Bureau of Economic Analysis

[1]Excludes Carribean financial centers

Even with the 2005 anomaly, U.S. investment flows to Europe considerably outweighed U.S. investment elsewhere. For example, while U.S. foreign direct investment to China has increased sharply over the past few years, total U.S. investment in China last year ($1.6 billion) was just 23% of total U.S. investment in Belgium in 2005. U.S. investment in Germany was roughly four-and-a-half times larger than U.S. investment in China in 2005. U.S. investment in France, while down due to the repatriation of U.S. reinvested earnings in 2005, was still some 16.7% greater than what U.S. firms invested in India.

Throughout this decade Europe has retained its position as the primary target of U.S. investment around the world. Between 2000 and 2005, U.S. companies invested more than four times as much in the UK than in China/Hong Kong. U.S. investments in China are accelerating, but from a low base. Over the course of this decade, U.S. investments in China/Hong Kong have been slightly less than U.S. investments in Ireland.

On a historic cost basis, the U.S. investment position in Europe was nearly three times larger than corporate America's investment position in all of Asia at the end of 2005. U.S. investment stakes in Italy at the end of 2005, some $26 billion on a historic cost basis, were greater than the combined U.S. investment position in China and India ($25.4 billion).

U.S. foreign affiliate sales in Europe hit a record $1.9 trillion in 2004, up from $1.6 trillion in the prior year. By a significant margin, Europe remains the top market in the world for U.S. affiliates, although the geographic distribution of affiliate sales has subtly shifted over the past few decades. In 2004, for instance, the share of U.S. foreign affiliate sales to the local market (as a percentage of the total) fell below 60% for the first time, dropping to 58.8%. In 1990, the share of U.S. affiliate sales to the local market was nearly 65%.

U.S. Affiliate Sales in Europe By Destination
% of total

	Calendar 1982 :			Calendar 1990 :			Calendar 2004 :		
Region	Local Market	Exports to 3rd Market	Exports to U.S.	Local Market	Exports to 3rd Market	Exports to U.S.	Local Market	Exports to 3rd Market	Exports to U.S.
World	**63.7%**	**25.6%**	**10.7%**	**67.0%**	**22.8%**	**10.2%**	**63.0%**	**26.6%**	**10.4%**
Europe	**61.4%**	**35.0%**	**3.6%**	**64.8%**	**31.2%**	**4.0%**	**58.8%**	**35.2%**	**6.0%**
Austria	na	na	na	77.8%	21.1%	1.1%	70.2%	27.7%	2.1%
Belgium	39.7%	57.2%	3.1%	41.5%	55.5%	3.0%	45.5%	50.8%	3.8%
Denmark	na	na	na	75.7%	20.0%	4.3%	66.5%	24.0%	9.5%
Finland	97.6%	na	na	97.4%	0.2%	2.4%	58.2%	38.9%	2.9%
France	74.1%	24.0%	1.9%	72.4%	24.6%	3.0%	74.8%	21.0%	4.1%
Germany	69.8%	28.1%	2.1%	68.4%	29.0%	2.6%	65.0%	31.4%	3.6%
Ireland	na	na	5.3%	29.3%	64.9%	5.8%	23.8%	60.8%	15.4%
Italy	83.0%	16.0%	1.0%	82.3%	16.2%	1.5%	79.8%	17.4%	2.8%
Netherlands	44.1%	53.0%	2.9%	41.8%	55.7%	2.5%	43.8%	49.9%	6.3%
Norway	45.7%	41.7%	12.6%		37.7%		63.1%	31.3%	5.6%
Portugal	76.6%	22.8%	0.6%	79.5%	20.1%	0.4%	76.2%	22.1%	1.6%
Spain	72.9%	25.8%	1.3%	74.7%	23.7%	1.6%	70.3%	28.1%	1.6%
Sweden	81.0%	18.1%	0.9%	78.8%	19.1%	2.1%	57.8%	32.0%	10.1%
Switzerland	12.4%	81.3%	6.3%	25.4%	63.5%	11.1%	18.4%	76.8%	4.8%
United Kingdom	68.3%	26.4%	5.3%	74.6%	20.3%	5.1%	71.1%	21.0%	7.8%

Source: Bureau of Economic Analysis

While local sales have declined as a percentage of the total, affiliate sales to the third markets has increased sharply. In effect, U.S. affiliates are increasingly leveraging some European nations as export platforms. Ireland is a prime example. There, U.S. foreign affiliates sales totaled $121 billion in 2004, making Ireland one of the largest markets in the EU in terms of foreign affiliate sales. However, foreign affiliate sales to the local market amounted to just $29 billion in 2004, or less than one-quarter of the total. Sales to third markets, however, represented 61% of the total, while affiliate sales to the U.S. accounted for nearly 16% of the total.

Belgium, the Netherlands and Switzerland are three other nations where U.S. affiliate sales are greater in third markets and the U.S. than in the local market. The same is true for Hungary, a low-cost center for production and distribution for many U.S. affiliates in the heart of Europe. The trend is also visible in Finland: in 1990 only 0.2% of Finnish-based U.S. affiliate sales were directed outside the local market; in 2004 38.9% was directed at third markets. A similar trend is noticeable in Sweden as well.

The accession of ten countries (Cyprus, Czech Republic, Estonia, Hungary, Lithuania, Latvia, Malta, Poland, Slovenia, and Slovakia) to the EU in 2004, along with the inclusion of Romania and Bulgaria at the start of 2007, presents a host of new and promising strategic opportunities for U.S. multinationals. Accession has integrated these nations into the mainstream of transatlantic commerce and expanded the size of the Single European Market. The last two rounds of enlargement has increased the number of EU member nations by over two-thirds, from 15 to 27; boosted the EU's population by more than 20%; and doubled both its territory and its official languages. While the 12 new members add only a bit more than 5% to the overall output of the EU, they have been registering annual growth rates in excess of the EU annual average. U.S. multinationals have been very active in the accession states over the past decade, and are already well integrated into central and eastern Europe.

More Globally Integrated: Inward FDI Stock as a Percentage of GDP

(%)

Country	1995	2005
Estonia	14.4	93.6
Malta	na	77.3
Hungary	26.7	55.9
Cyprus	na	52.7
Czech Republic	14.1	48.1
Slovakia	4.4	32.8
Poland	6.2	31.1
Latvia	12.5	28.7
Lithuania	5.8	25.1
Slovenia	8.3	23.7
World	10.3	22.7

Source: United Nations

In particular, U.S. multinationals have been the focused on the "Big Three" accession states—Poland, Hungary and the Czech Republic. In 2005, these three nations together accounted for over 85% of total U.S. investment in the 10 nations admitted into the EU in 2004. In terms of profits—or affiliate income—U.S. affiliates earned $1.5 billion in the "Big Three" in 2005, some 36% more than what affiliates earned in India, a much over-hyped market of over 1 billion people. Between 2000 and 2005, combined affiliate income from Poland, Hungary and the Czech Republic nearly tripled, underscoring the fact that central Europe has rapidly become a new source of revenue for many U.S. firms.

European affiliates of U.S. companies are major employers in many European nations. Affiliates directly employ more than 1 million workers in the UK; 601,700 in Germany; 562,800 in France; 238,500 in Italy; 197,200 in Spain; 120,000 in Belgium. The U.S. affiliate work force in Poland has grown from a modest level a decade ago to 90,700 – among the largest in all of Europe. As we have mentioned in earlier chapters, these figures tend to understate total employment levels, because they do not include indirect employment related to non-equity arrangements such as strategic alliances, joint ventures and other deals. Moreover, affiliate employment figures do not include jobs supported by transatlantic trade, which are also substantial.

America's Foreign Investment in EU Accession Countries

($U.S. billions, 2005)

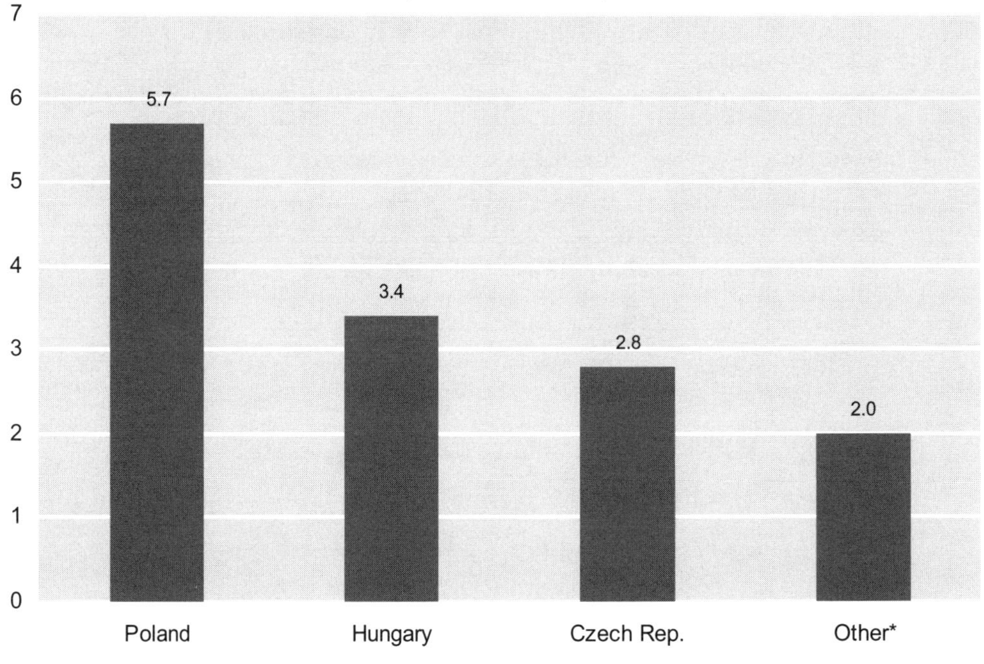

Source: Bureau of Economic Analysis

*Cyprus, Estonia, Latvia, Lithuania, Malta, Slovakia, Slovenia

U.S. Foreign Affiliate Sales in the EU Accession "Big Three" Countries
($U.S. billions, 2004)

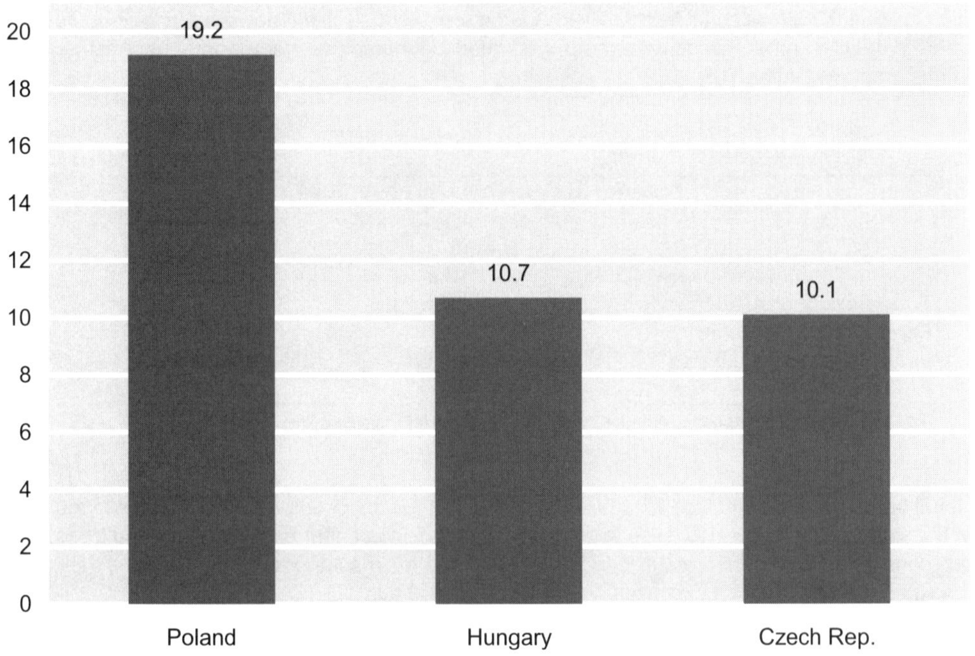

Source: Bureau of Economic Analysis

The following pages outline U.S.-sourced jobs, trade and investment for each of the members of the European Union, including new member states, Bulgaria and Romania. Norway and Switzerland are also included.

Austria & the United States
Investment and Trade Figures

Investment

Not surprisingly, America's investment position in Austria exceeds Austria's investment stakes in the U.S. At $15.5 billion in 2004, U.S. foreign affiliate sales in Austria were roughly five times greater than comparable affiliate sales in the U.S. American affiliates employed nearly four times as many workers in Austria than Austrian firms employed in the U.S.

Austria - U.S. Global Linkages, 2004
($ billions)

	U.S. in Austria	Austria in U.S.
Foreign Direct Investment* (2005)	8.8	2.5
Total Assets of Affiliates	25.5	2.2
Foreign Affiliate Sales	15.5	2.9
Value Added of Affiliates	4.6	0.7
Affiliate Employees	33,300	9,600

*Based on a historic-cost basis, data for 2005; gross product for majority-owned affiliates

Trade

On a global basis, the U.S. received $7.3 billion, or 5.8% of the total goods Austria exported to the world in 2005, but the share going to the U.S. rises to 19.3% of the global total after excluding intra-EU trade. Imports of U.S. goods constituted $2.8 billion, or 2.2% of the total amount Austria imported from the world the same year and 10.6% when intra-EU imports were removed from the global total.

Top Ten U.S. Imports from Austria, 2005 (in $ millions)

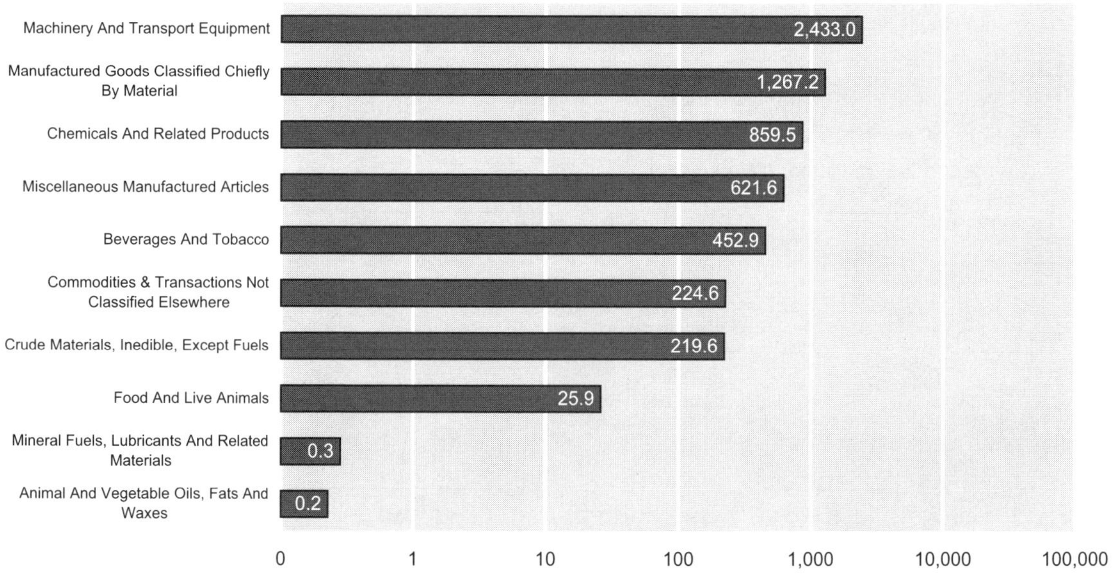

Source: Bureau of Economic Analysis, International Monetary Fund; Office of Trade and Industry Information

Belgium & the United States

Investment and Trade Figures

Investment

America's investment position in Belgium is nearly four times larger than Belgium's investment stakes in the U.S. However, Belgium affiliates employed nearly 9% more workers in the U.S. than U.S. affiliates in Belgium. Value added by U.S. affiliates in Belgium totaled $18.3 billion in 2004, nearly 40% greater than U.S. affiliate output in China.

Belgium - U.S. Global Linkages, 2004
($ billions)

	U.S. in Belgium	Belgium in U.S.
Foreign Direct Investment* (2005)	36.7	9.7
Total Assets of Affiliates	225.5	78.5
Foreign Affiliate Sales	72.1	31.4
Value Added of Affiliates	18.3	7.9
Affiliate Employees	120,000	130,400

*Based on a historic-cost basis, data for 2005; gross product for majority-owned affiliates

Trade

The U.S. accounted for 6.4% of total exports from Belgium in 2005, but a share of 27.2% of total exports when intra-EU trade is excluded. Manufactured goods lead the way as the top export category. Regarding imports, the U.S. supplied 5.4% of total imports by Belgium in 2005, although the share rises to 18.9% after accounting for intra-EU trade.

Top Ten U.S. Imports from Belgium, 2005 (in $ millions)

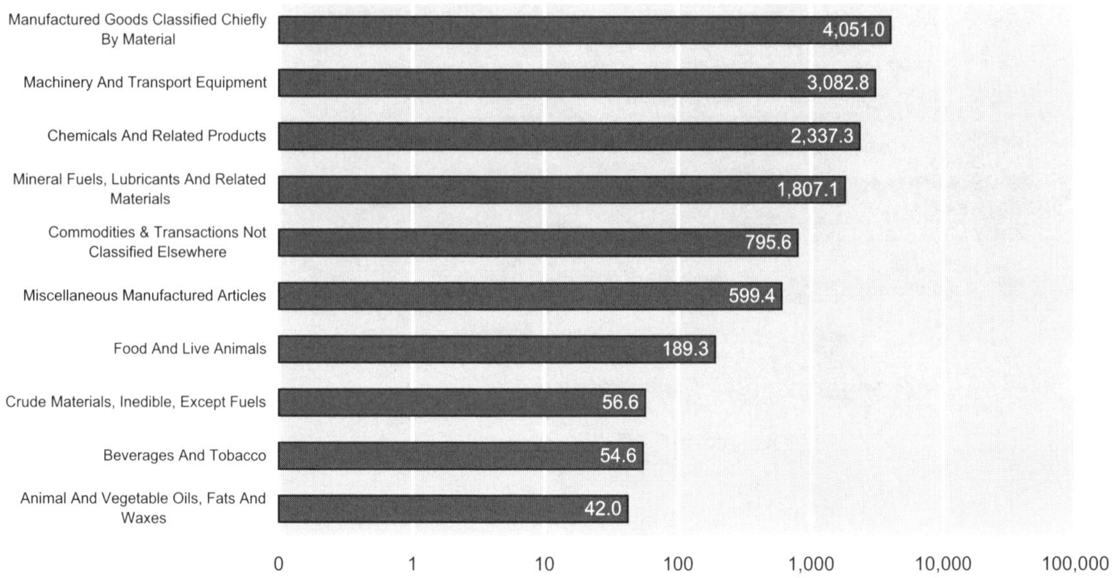

Source: Bureau of Economic Analysis, International Monetary Fund; Office of Trade and Industry Information

Bulgaria & the United States
Investment and Trade Figures

Investment
America's investment base in Bulgaria is rather small, with U.S. investment totaling just $100 million in 2005.

Bulgaria - U.S. Global Linkages, 2004 ($ billions)	U.S. in Bulgaria	Bulgaria in U.S.
Foreign Direct Investment* (2005)	0.1	-
Total Assets of Affiliates	0.5	-
Foreign Affiliate Sales	0.4	-
Value Added of Affiliates	0.1	-
Affiliate Employees	5,700	-

*Based on a historic-cost basis, data for 2005; gross product for majority-owned affiliates

Trade
The U.S. accounted for just 3% of Bulgaria's total exports in 2005; the percentage rises to just 6.9% when intra-EU trade is excluded from the total. Imports from the U.S. are rather small, totaling just $500 million in 2005.

Top Ten U.S. Imports from Bulgaria, 2005 (in $ millions)

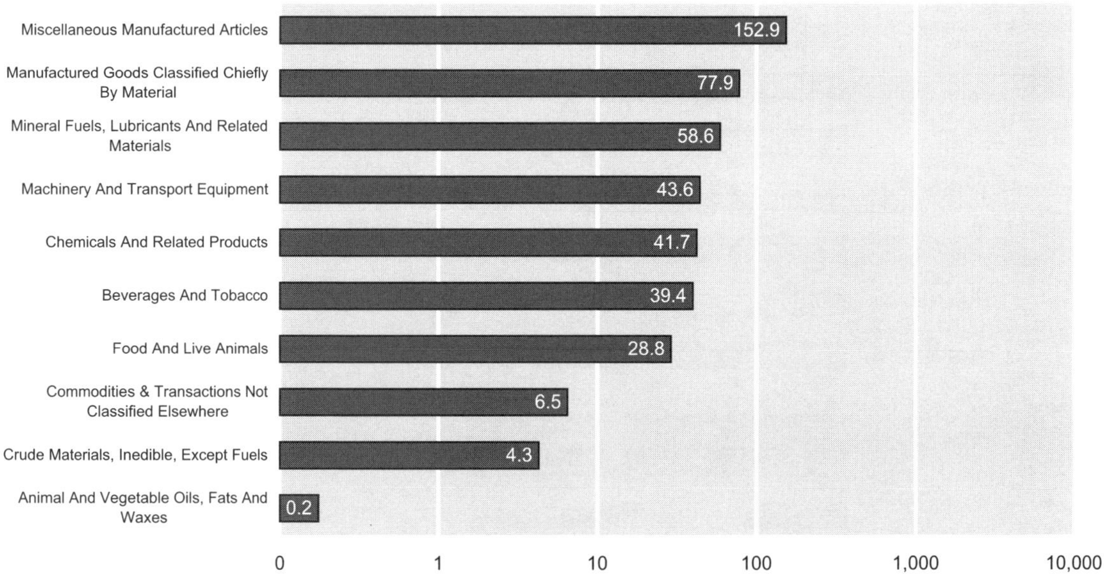

Source: Bureau of Economic Analysis, International Monetary Fund; Office of Trade and Industry Information

Cyprus & the United States

Investment and Trade Figures

Investment

Given the ongoing political uncertainty in Cyprus, and the country's small market, the nation has not attracted much in the way of U.S. foreign direct investment.

Cyprus - U.S. Global Linkages, 2004 ($ billions)	U.S. in Cyprus	Cyprus in U.S.
Foreign Direct Investment* (2005)	0.2	-
Total Assets of Affiliates	1.1	-
Foreign Affiliate Sales	0.7	-
Value Added of Affiliates	0.2	-
Affiliate Employees	500	-

*Based on a historic-cost basis, data for 2005; gross product for majority-owned affiliates

Trade

Cyprus is an insignificant supplier of goods to the United States; the U.S. accounted for just 1.4 % of total exports in 2005. Imports from the U.S. were quite small in 2005, totaling $100 million.

Top Ten U.S. Imports from Cyprus, 2005 (in $ millions)

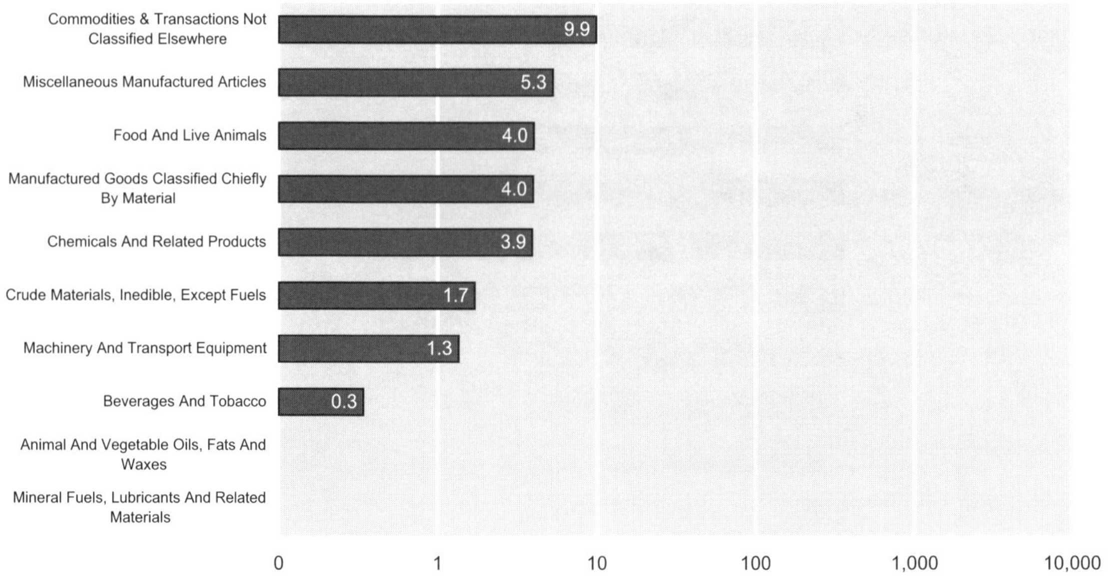

Source: Bureau of Economic Analysis, International Monetary Fund; Office of Trade and Industry Information

Czech Republic & the United States

Investment and Trade Figures

Investment

America's investment base in the Czech Republic is small but expanding, owing to the nation's skilled labor pool and low wages. U.S. foreign direct investment totaled $2.8 billion on a historic cost basis in 2005. Value added by U.S.-owned affiliates totaled $3.0 billion. Affiliate employment in the Czech Republic (60,300 workers) is among the highest in Eastern Europe. Not surprisingly, there is virtually no foreign investment from the Czech Republic in the U.S.

Czech Republic - U.S. Global Linkages, 2004
($ billions)

	U.S. in Czech Republic	Czech Republic in U.S.
Foreign Direct Investment* (2005)	2.8	-
Total Assets of Affiliates	9.3	-
Foreign Affiliate Sales	9.6	-
Value Added of Affiliates	3.0	-
Affiliate Employees	60,300	-

*Based on a historic-cost basis, data for 2005; gross product for majority-owned affiliates

Trade

U.S. imports from the Czech Republic totaled $2.0 billion in 2005, having nearly tripled since 1997. Imports consist of high-end goods like parts and components for nuclear reactors and electronic machinery.

Top Ten U.S. Imports from Czech Republic, 2005 (in $ millions)

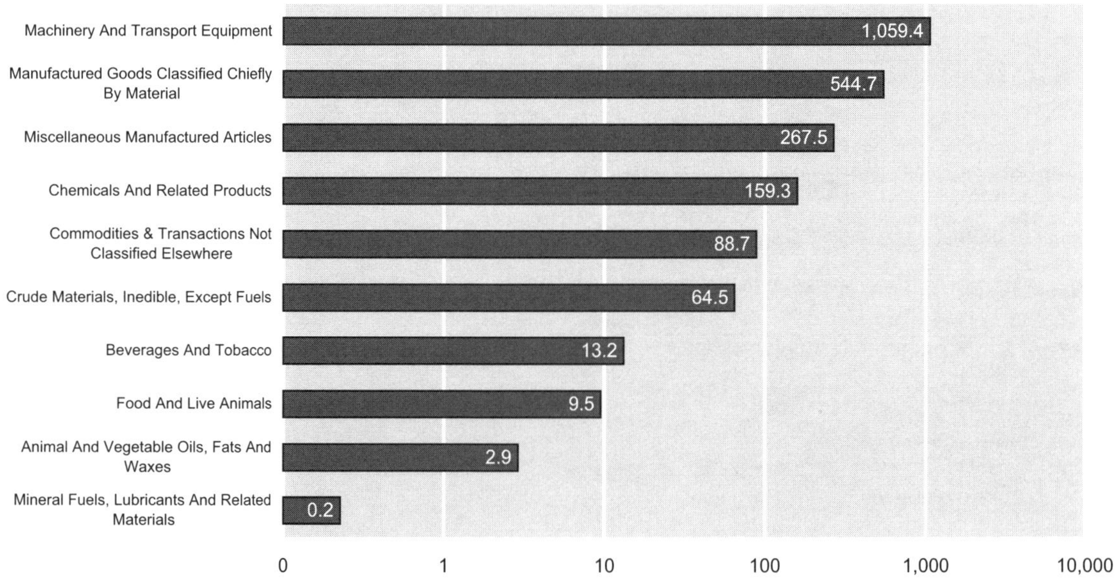

Source: Bureau of Economic Analysis, International Monetary Fund; Office of Trade and Industry Information

Denmark & the United States

Investment and Trade Figures

Investment

Bilateral investment between the U.S. and Denmark is surprisingly balanced given Denmark's small size. Danish investment in the U.S. totaled $6.3 billion in 2005, while U.S. investment in Denmark approached $ 6 billion; affiliate sales in the U.S. market approached $10.3 billion in 2004. The affiliate employment balance favors the United States.

Denmark - U.S. Global Linkages, 2004

($ billions)

	U.S. in Denmark	Denmark in U.S.
Foreign Direct Investment* (2005)	5.7	6.3
Total Assets of Affiliates	46.9	21.1
Foreign Affiliate Sales	12.3	10.3
Value Added of Affiliates	5.5	3.3
Affiliate Employees	38,300	60,600

*Based on a historic-cost basis, data for 2005; gross product for majority-owned affiliates

Trade

Exports from Denmark to the U.S. totaled $5.5 billion in 2004, or 6.4% of the global total. Excluding intra-EU trade, the share of exports to the U.S. rises to 21.4%. Danish imports from the U.S. totaled $2.1 billion the same year, 2.7% of the global total and 9.4% ex. intra-EU trade.

Top Ten U.S. Imports from Denmark, 2005 (in $ millions)

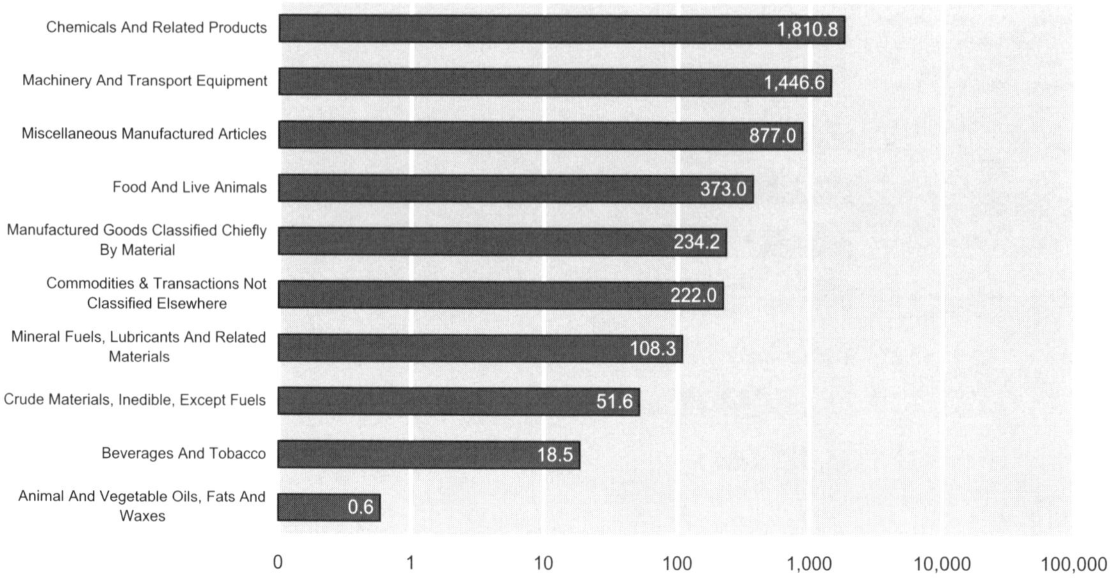

Source: Bureau of Economic Analysis, International Monetary Fund; Office of Trade and Industry Information

Estonia & the United States
Investment and Trade Figures

Investment

America's investment base in Estonia is rather small but expected to expand as the Baltic states emerge as a key gateway to Russia and beyond.

Estonia - U.S. Global Linkages, 2004 ($ billions)	U.S. in Estonia	Estonia in U.S.
Foreign Direct Investment* (2005)	0.0	-
Total Assets of Affiliates	0.2	-
Foreign Affiliate Sales	0.2	-
Value Added of Affiliates	0.1	-
Affiliate Employees	1,700	-

*Based on a historic-cost basis, data for 2005; gross product for majority-owned affiliates

Trade

U.S. imports from Estonia totaled $200 million in 2005, in line with levels of 2003 ($181 million) but well off the peak levels of 2000, when imports topped $500 million. The decline reflects the fall in U.S. imports of mineral fuel during the past few years.

Top Ten U.S. Imports from Estonia, 2005 (in $ millions)

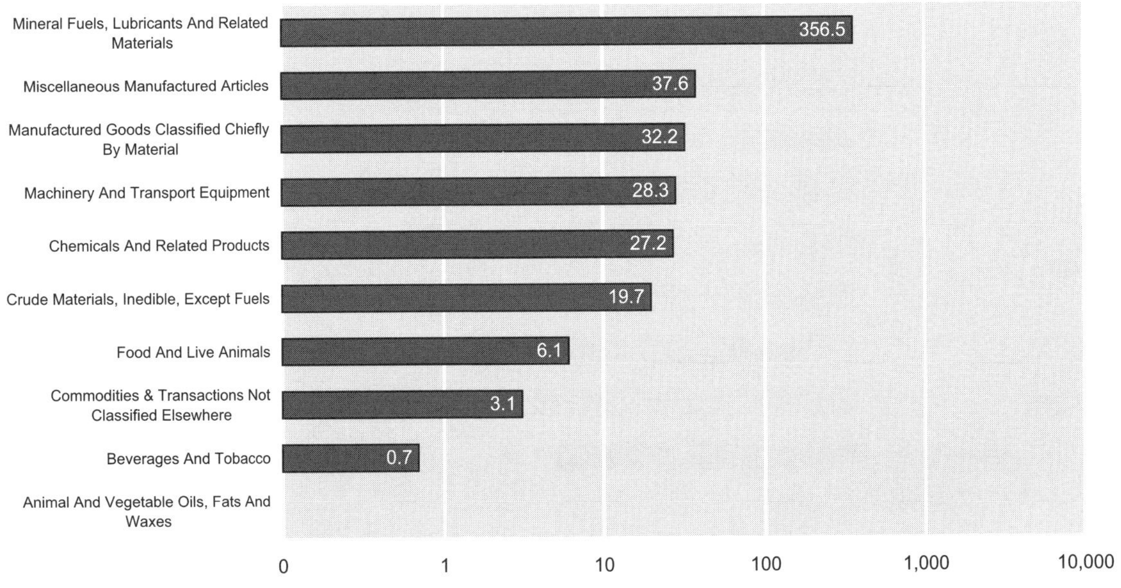

Source: Bureau of Economic Analysis, International Monetary Fund; Office of Trade and Industry Information

Finland & the United States
Investment and Trade Figures

Investment

The investment balance favors the United States, with Finnish investment in the U.S. totaling $6.2 billion in 2005 versus just $2.5 billion of U.S. investment in Finland. A larger investment presence benefited Finnish affiliate sales in the U.S., which were some 80% larger than U.S. affiliate sales in Finland. The affiliate employment balance favors the U.S.

Finland - U.S. Global Linkages, 2004 ($ billions)	U.S. in Finland	Finland in U.S.
Foreign Direct Investment* (2005)	2.5	6.2
Total Assets of Affiliates	12.6	13.8
Foreign Affiliate Sales	10.1	18.5
Value Added of Affiliates	2.9	3.8
Affiliate Employees	19,600	36,200

*Based on a historic-cost basis, data for 2005; gross product for majority-owned affiliates

Trade

The U.S. received $4.1 billion, or 6.2% of the total goods Finland exported to the world in 2005, but the share going to the U.S. rises to 14.1% of the global total after excluding intra-EU trade. Imports of U.S. goods constituted $2 billion, or 3.5% of the total amount Finland imported from the world the same year and 10.1% when intra-EU imports were removed from the global total.

Top Ten U.S. Imports from Finland, 2005 (in $ millions)

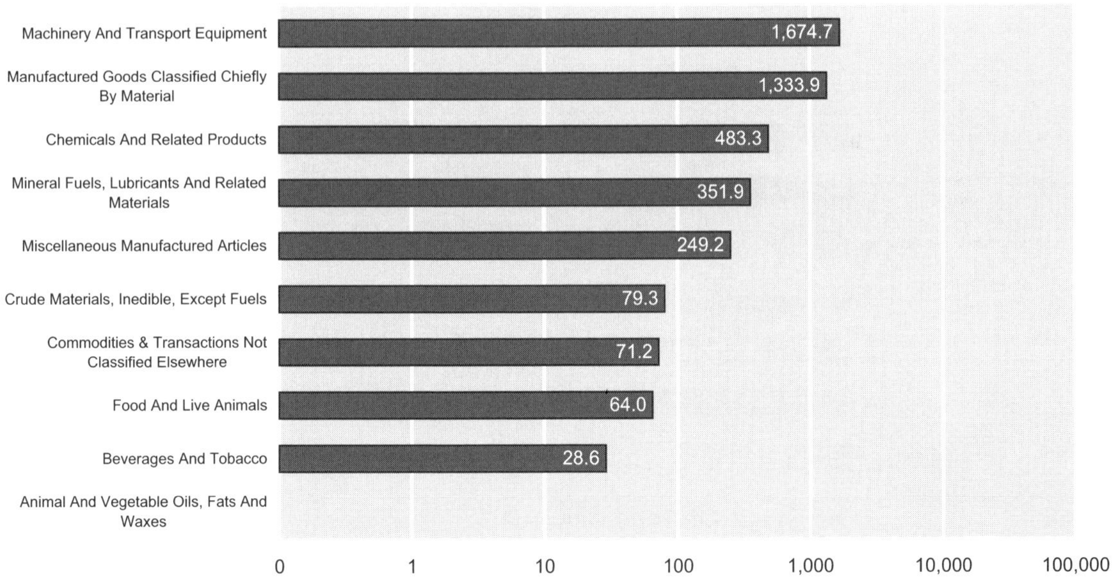

Source: Bureau of Economic Analysis, International Monetary Fund; Office of Trade and Industry Information

France & the United States

Investment and Trade Figures

Investment

The investment balance favors the U.S., with U.S. investment in France ($60.9 billion) just 42% of total French investment in the U.S. in 2005 ($143.4 billion). The U.S. is a significant market for French firms, with U.S. affiliates of French firms recording nearly $172 billion in sales during 2004. France now receives the advantage in the affiliate employment balance. U.S. and French affiliates combined employed over 1 million workers in 2004.

France - U.S. Global Linkages, 2004
($ billions)

	U.S. in France	France in U.S.
Foreign Direct Investment* (2005)	60.9	143.4
Total Assets of Affiliates	235.4	596.6
Foreign Affiliate Sales	163.0	172.4
Value Added of Affiliates	47.7	43.1
Affiliate Employees	562,800	451,600

*Based on a historic-cost basis, data for 2005; gross product for majority-owned affiliates

Trade

The U.S. accounted for 7.2% of total exports from France in 2005, but a share of 19.1% of total exports when intra-EU trade is excluded. Products exported to the U.S. ran the gamut, from heavy machinery and transportation equipment to agricultural products. Regarding imports, the U.S. supplied 5.1% of total imports by France in 2005, although the share rises to 15.3% after accounting for intra-EU trade.

Top Ten U.S. Imports from France, 2005 (in $ millions)

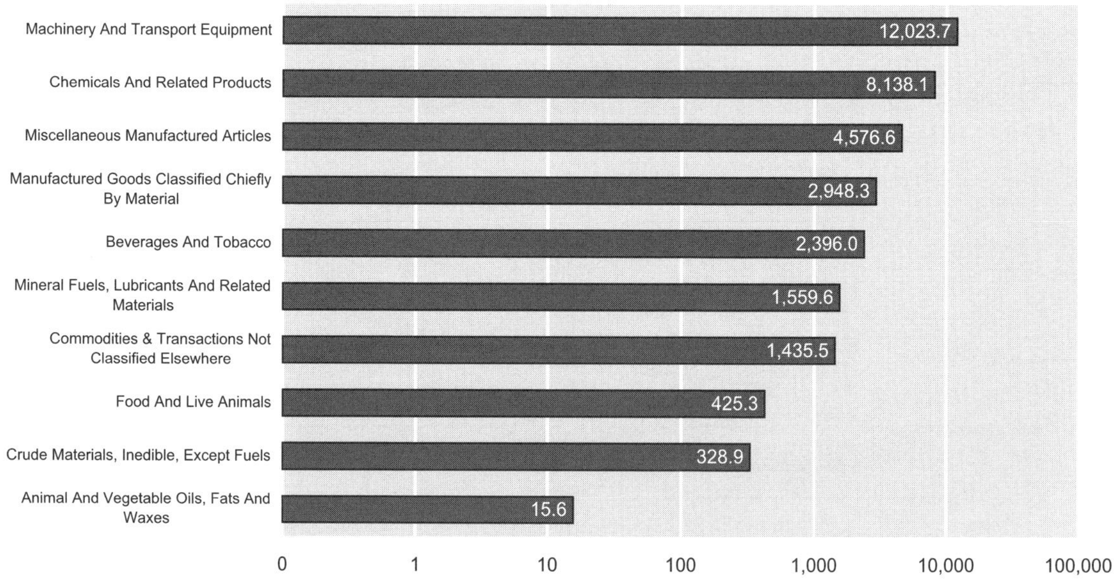

Source: Bureau of Economic Analysis, International Monetary Fund; Office of Trade and Industry Information

Germany & the United States

Investment and Trade Figures

Investment

The investment balance favors the U.S., with U.S. investment in Germany totaling $86.3 billion in 2005 versus $184.2 billion of German investment in the U.S. Germany's asset base in the U.S. exceeded America's total asset base in Germany by two-thirds in 2004, although the value added by American affiliates operating in Germany ($74.2 billion in 2004) exceeded that of German affiliates in the United States. The employment balance favored the U.S. in 2004. U.S. and German affiliates combined employed over 1.2 million workers.

Germany - U.S. Global Linkages, 2004

($ billions)

	U.S. in Germany	Germany in U.S.
Foreign Direct Investment* (2005)	86.3	184.2
Total Assets of Affiliates	378.8	632.1
Foreign Affiliate Sales	252.1	319.7
Value Added of Affiliates	74.2	66.4
Affiliate Employees	601,700	668,600

*Based on a historic-cost basis, data for 2005; gross product for majority-owned affiliates

Trade

Germany is the largest European exporter to the U.S., with exports to the U.S. totaling over $86.1 billion in 2005. The U.S. accounted for just over 8.8% of total German exports, but roughly 24% when intra-EU trade flows are excluded. Imports from the U.S. into Germany totaled $51.4 billion—that equates to 6.6% of total German imports or 16.1% excluding intra-EU trade.

Top Ten U.S. Imports from Germany, 2005 (in $ millions)

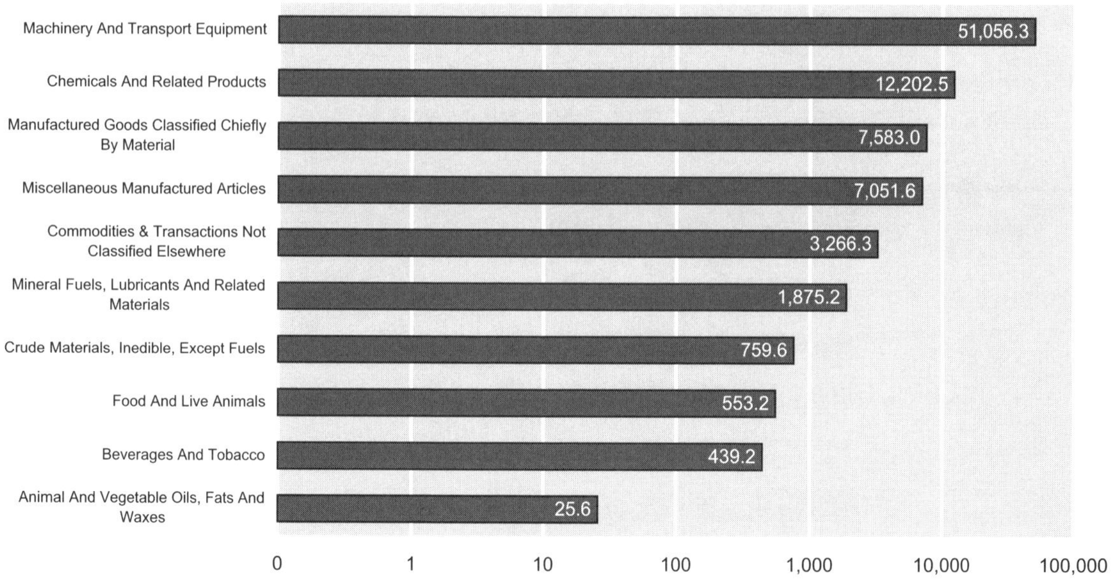

Source: Bureau of Economic Analysis, International Monetary Fund; Office of Trade and Industry Information

Greece & the United States
Investment and Trade Figures

Investment

America's investment position in Greece is rather small, totaling just $1.9 billion in 2005. No data is available regarding the investment position of Greece in the U.S. U.S. affiliate sales of just $6.2 billion in 2004 ranked among the lowest in the EU.

Greece - U.S. Global Linkages, 2004 ($ billions)	U.S. in Greece	Greece in U.S.
Foreign Direct Investment* (2005)	1.9	-
Total Assets of Affiliates	7.8	-
Foreign Affiliate Sales	6.2	-
Value Added of Affiliates	2.8	-
Affiliate Employees	15,800	-

*Based on a historic-cost basis, data for 2005; gross product for majority-owned affiliates

Trade

Greek exports to the U.S. totaled just $900 million in 2005, while imports from the U.S. amounted to $1.9 billion. The U.S. accounted for 5.3% of total exports but nearly 11.3% ex. intra-EU exports. Greek imports from the U.S. were 3.5% of total imports from the world in 2004 and 8% ex. intra-EU imports.

Top Ten U.S. Imports from Greece, 2005 (in $ millions)

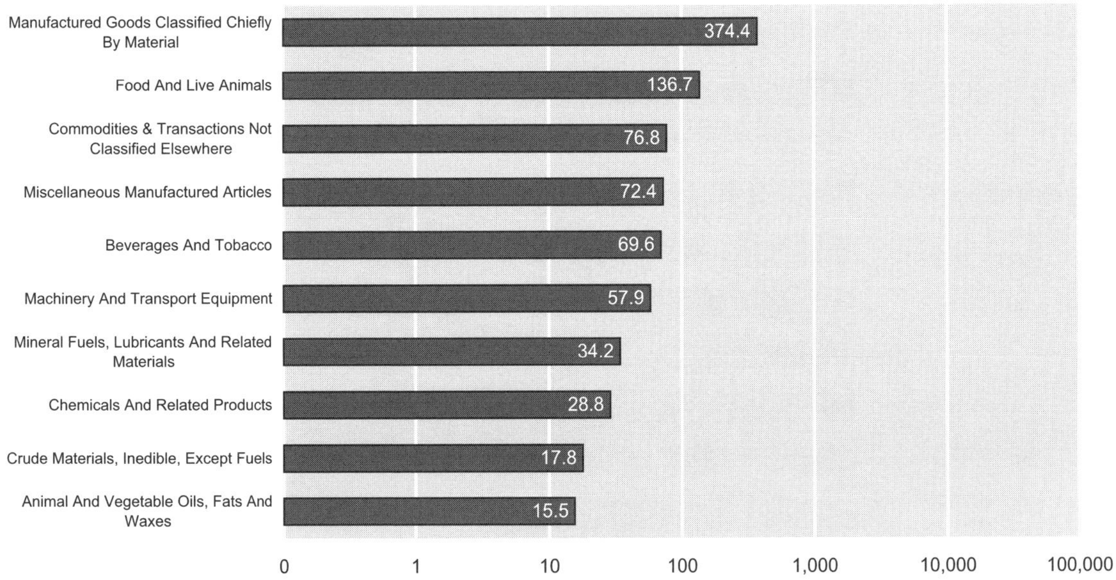

Source: Bureau of Economic Analysis, International Monetary Fund; Office of Trade and Industry Information

Hungary & the United States
Investment and Trade Figures

Investment

America's investment base in Hungary is among the largest in central Europe, with U.S. foreign direct investment totaling $3.4 billion on a historic cost basis in 2005. Value added by U.S.-owned affiliates totaled $2.3 billion. Affiliate employment in Hungary (51,300 workers) was well beyond the number of workers employed next door in Austria. Hungary's investment position in the U.S. is limited.

Hungary - U.S. Global Linkages, 2004 ($ billions)	U.S. in Hungary	Hungary in U.S.
Foreign Direct Investment* (2005)	3.4	-
Total Assets of Affiliates	16.5	-
Foreign Affiliate Sales	10.1	-
Value Added of Affiliates	2.3	-
Affiliate Employees	51,300	-

*Based on a historic-cost basis, data for 2005; gross product for majority-owned affiliates

Trade

U.S. imports from Hungary totaled $1.9 billion in 2005, up from $1.8 billion in 1997. The bulk of imports consists of parts and components, including those used in nuclear reactors. Vehicle and electronic shipments have increased along with greater affiliate production in the country. Hungary bought $1.1 billion of U.S. goods in 2005.

Top Ten U.S. Imports from Hungary, 2005 (in $ millions)

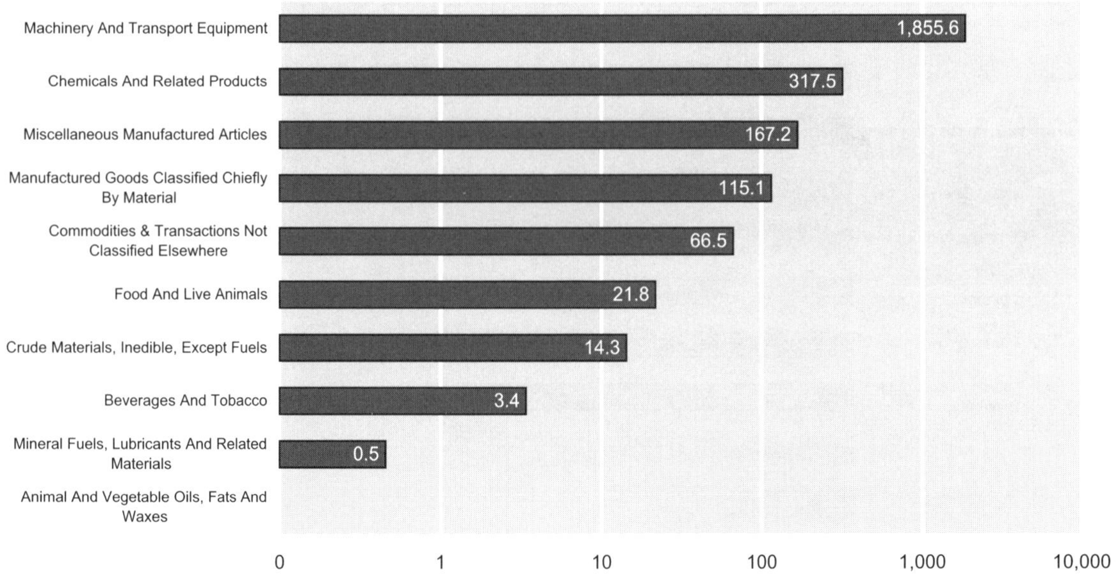

Source: Bureau of Economic Analysis, International Monetary Fund; Office of Trade and Industry Information

Ireland & the United States

Investment and Trade Figures

Investment

The investment balance favors Ireland, with U.S. investment in Ireland totaling some $61.6 billion in 2005 versus $21.9 billion of Ireland's investment in the U.S. Value added by U.S. affiliates totaled $27.0 billion in 2004. The affiliate employment balance favors Ireland by roughly 45,000 jobs. In particular, U.S. technology firms continue to build out their presence in Ireland.

Ireland - U.S. Global Linkages, 2004

($ billions)

	U.S. in Ireland	Ireland in U.S.
Foreign Direct Investment* (2005)	61.6	21.9
Total Assets of Affiliates	276.5	17.6
Foreign Affiliate Sales	121.2	12.4
Value Added of Affiliates	27.0	3.7
Affiliate Employees	82,800	37,400

*Based on a historic-cost basis, data for 2005; gross product for majority-owned affiliates

Trade

The U.S. is key export destination for Ireland, with exports to the U.S. totaling $20.6 billion in 2005. The U.S. accounted for 18.7% of total exports from Ireland; when intra-EU exports are excluded from the total, the share of exports to the U.S. jumps to 51%. Top exports to the U.S. include machinery and manufactured products. The U.S. is also a key supplier to Ireland, with the U.S. accounting for 9.5% of total imports into Ireland in 2005 and 39% after excluding intra-EU trade.

Top Ten U.S. Imports from Ireland, 2005 (in $ millions)

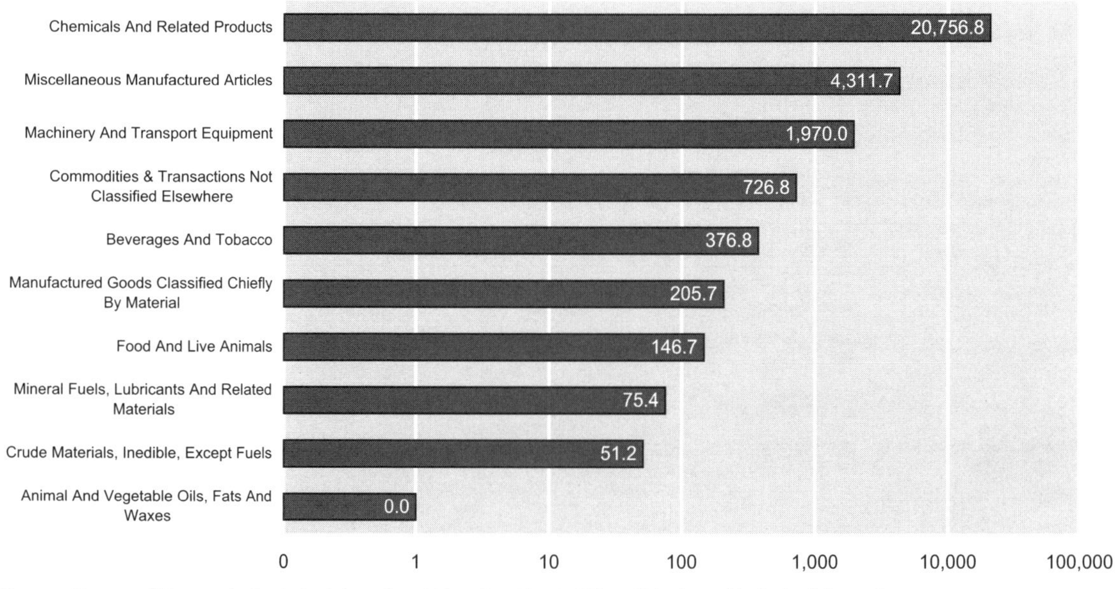

Source: Bureau of Economic Analysis, International Monetary Fund; Office of Trade and Industry Information

Italy & the United States
Investment and Trade Figures

Investment

The investment balance favors Italy—U.S. investment in Italy totaled $25.9 billion in 2005, versus the $7.7 billion invested by Italian firms in the U.S. Value added by U.S. affiliates in Italy was nearly five times as much as that produced by Italian affiliates in the U.S. With U.S. foreign affiliates employing some 238,500 workers in 2004, the employment balance clearly favors Italy.

Italy - U.S. Global Linkages, 2004
($ billions)

	U.S. in Italy	Italy in U.S.
Foreign Direct Investment* (2005)	25.9	7.7
Total Assets of Affiliates	105.4	38.9
Foreign Affiliate Sales	99.1	23.7
Value Added of Affiliates	29.3	6.2
Affiliate Employees	238,500	102,400

*Based on a historic-cost basis, data for 2005; gross product for majority-owned affiliates

Trade

The U.S. accounted for 8.1% of total exports from Italy in 2005, but a share of 19.6% of total exports after excluding intra-EU trade. Machinery, transportation goods, and manufactured goods were the top exports to the U.S. Regarding imports, the U.S. supplied 3.5% of total imports by Italy in 2005, although the share rises to 8.2% after accounting for intra-EU imports.

Top Ten U.S. Imports from Italy, 2005 (in $ millions)

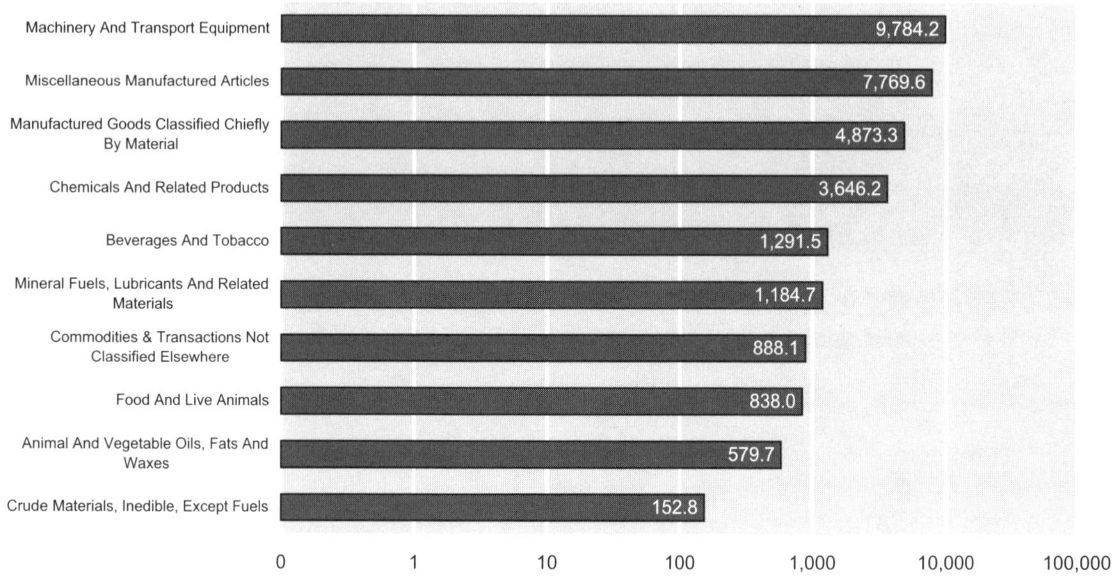

Source: Bureau of Economic Analysis, International Monetary Fund; Office of Trade and Industry Information

Latvia & the United States

Investment and Trade Figures

Investment

Latvia has yet to attract much foreign direct investment from the United States. Investment linkages are shallow but expected to gradually expand over the next decade. The nation is well positioned to serve as an export bridge to Russia.

Latvia - U.S. Global Linkages, 2004 ($ billions)	U.S. in Latvia	Latvia in U.S.
Foreign Direct Investment* (2005)	0.0	-
Total Assets of Affiliates	0.0	-
Foreign Affiliate Sales	0.0	-
Value Added of Affiliates	0.0	-
Affiliate Employees	600	-

*Based on a historic-cost basis, data for 2005; gross product for majority-owned affiliates

Trade

U.S. imports from Latvia have increased steadily over the past few years, with imports consisting mainly of primary commodities like mineral fuels, chemicals, iron and steel. The U.S. is a small supplier to Latvia, with U.S. exports totaling just $100 million in 2005.

Top Ten U.S. Imports from Latvia, 2005 (in $ millions)

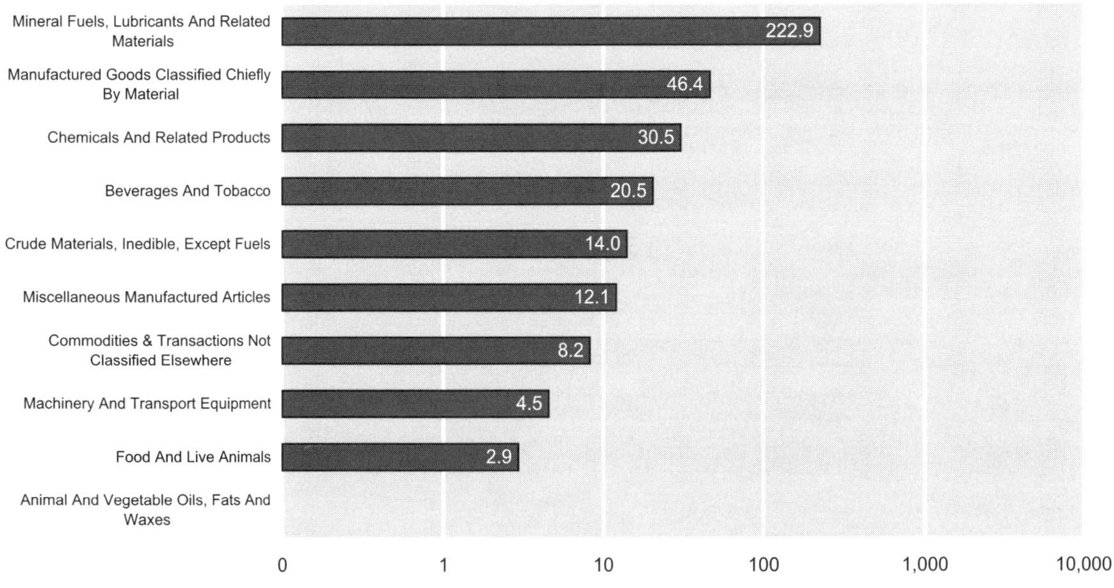

Source: Bureau of Economic Analysis, International Monetary Fund; Office of Trade and Industry Information

Lithuania & the United States
Investment and Trade Figures

Investment

Lithuania has yet to attract significant levels of U.S. foreign direct investment. However, as the Baltic states develop and become more integrated into the greater European market, U.S. investment flows are expected to increase.

Lithuania - U.S. Global Linkages, 2004 ($ billions)	U.S. in Lithuania	Lithuania in U.S.
Foreign Direct Investment* (2005)	0.0	-
Total Assets of Affiliates	0.0	-
Foreign Affiliate Sales	0.0	-
Value Added of Affiliates	0.1	-
Affiliate Employees	1,300	-

*Based on a historic-cost basis, data for 2005; gross product for majority-owned affiliates

Trade

U.S. imports from Lithuania have soared over the past decade, rising from just $79 million in 1997 to nearly $600 million in 2005. Rising shipments of mineral fuel led the import surge.

Top Ten U.S. Imports from Lithuania, 2005 (in $ millions)

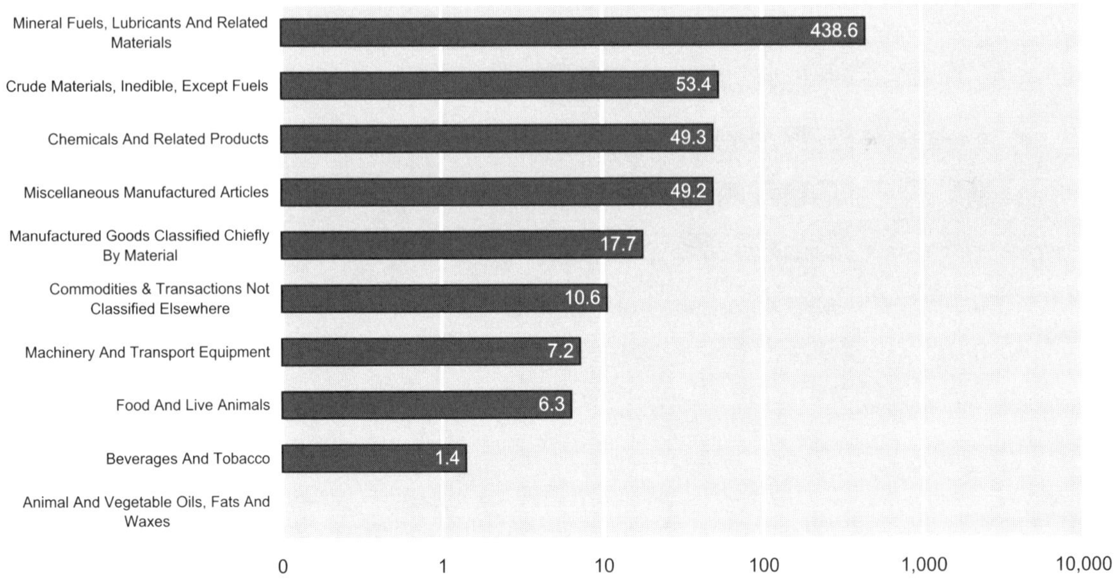

Source: Bureau of Economic Analysis, International Monetary Fund; Office of Trade and Industry Information

Luxembourg & the United States
Investment and Trade Figures

Investment

Investment between the U.S. and Luxembourg is skewed in favor of America, partially because most U.S. investment in Luxembourg is indirectly tied to other nations. The bulk of bilateral investment flows is in financial services and related industries.

Luxembourg - U.S. Global Linkages, 2004 ($ billions)	U.S. in Luxembourg	Luxembourg in U.S.
Foreign Direct Investment* (2005)	61.6	116.7
Total Assets of Affiliates	474.8	7.0
Foreign Affiliate Sales	10.7	3.1
Value Added of Affiliates	-0.6	1.1
Affiliate Employees	9,800	14,800

*Based on a historic-cost basis, data for 2005; gross product for majority-owned affiliates

Trade

Trade volumes are small—with exports to the U.S. totaling just $400 million in 2005, while imports from the U.S. amounted to $700 million. The U.S. accounted for only 2.1% of total exports but for nearly 14.6% ex. intra-EU exports. Imports from the U.S. accounted for 3.1% of the total in 2005 and 11.5% ex. intra-EU imports.

Top Ten U.S. Imports from Luxembourg, 2005 (in $ millions)

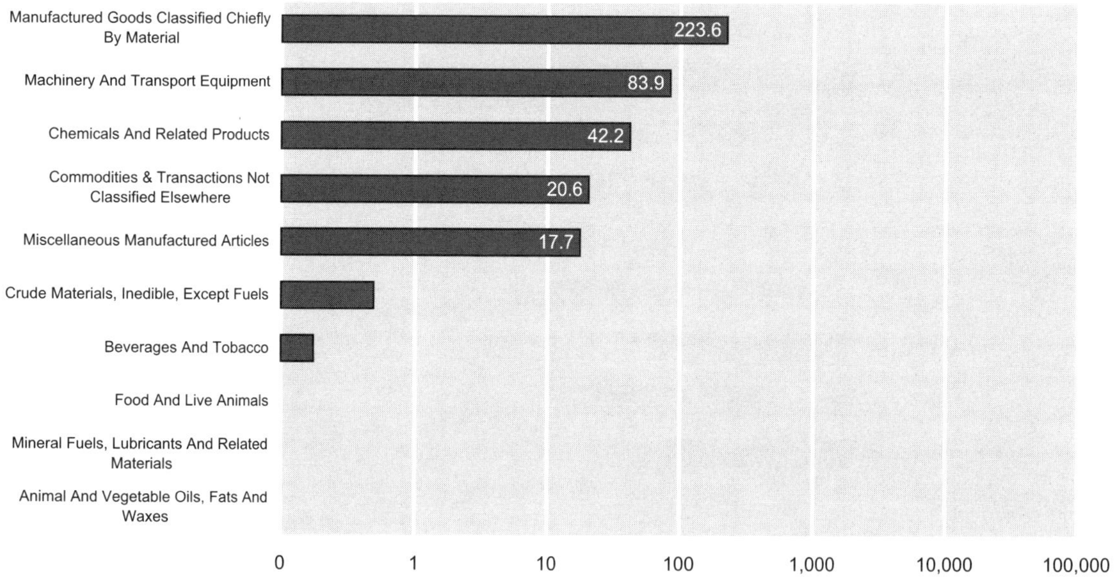

Source: Bureau of Economic Analysis, International Monetary Fund; Office of Trade and Industry Information

Malta & the United States
Investment and Trade Figures

Investment

Given its small size, Malta has not attracted much U.S. foreign direct investment over the past few decades.

Malta - U.S. Global Linkages, 2004 ($ billions)	U.S. in Malta	Malta in U.S.
Foreign Direct Investment* (2005)	0.1	-
Total Assets of Affiliates	1.3	-
Foreign Affiliate Sales	0.1	-
Value Added of Affiliates	0.0	-
Affiliate Employees	1,200	-

*Based on a historic-cost basis, data for 2005; gross product for majority-owned affiliates

Trade

U.S. imports from Malta totaled $300 million in 2005 and were primarily concentrated in electronic machinery and other manufactured items.

Top Ten U.S. Imports from Malta, 2005 (in $ millions)

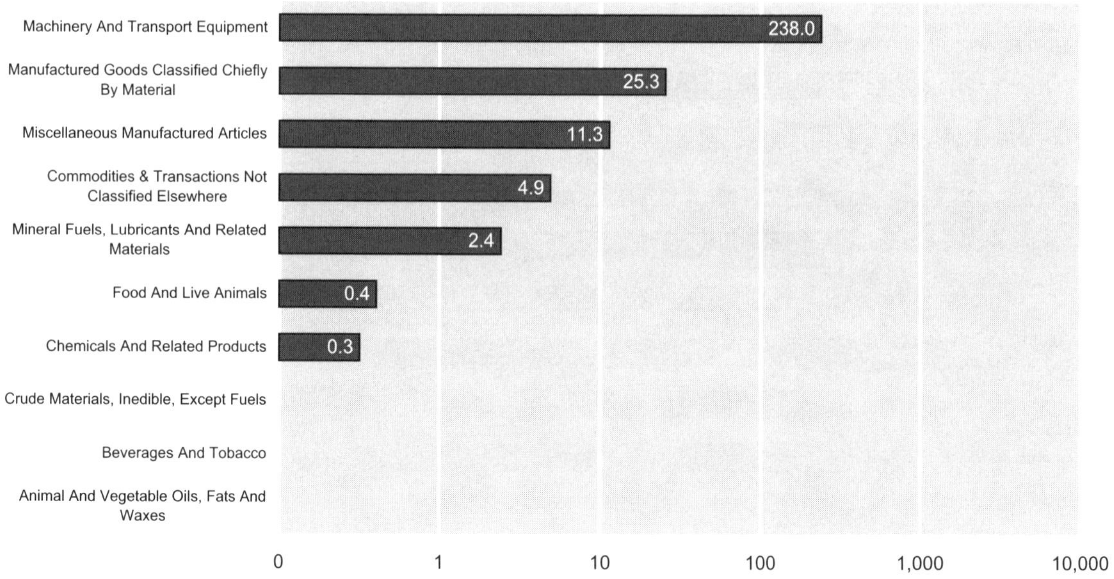

Source: Bureau of Economic Analysis, International Monetary Fund; Office of Trade and Industry Information

Netherlands & the United States

Investment and Trade Figures

Investment

Investment between the U.S. and the Netherlands is fairly balanced, with America's investment stake in the Netherlands totaling $181.4 billion in 2005, versus $170.8 billion of Dutch investment in the U.S. The U.S. is a prime foreign destination for Dutch firms, who recorded $224.9 billion in affiliate sales in the U.S. during 2004. That was roughly 60% of the amount U.S. affiliates sold in the Netherlands the same year. The employment balance favors the U.S. by a wide margin (more than 300,000 jobs).

Netherlands - U.S. Global Linkages, 2004
($ billions)

	U.S. in Netherlands	Netherlands in U.S.
Foreign Direct Investment* (2005)	181.4	170.8
Total Assets of Affiliates	693.2	574.9
Foreign Affiliate Sales	140.0	224.9
Value Added of Affiliates	28.2	43.8
Affiliate Employees	175,100	481,100

*Based on a historic-cost basis, data for 2005; gross product for majority-owned affiliates

Trade

The U.S. accounted for 4.3% of total exports from the Netherlands in 2005, but a share of 20.6% of total exports when intra-EU trade is excluded. Top exports were diversified across several capital-intensive industries. Regarding imports, the U.S. supplied 7.6% of total imports by the Netherlands in 2005, although the share rises to 14.9% after accounting for intra-EU trade.

Top Ten U.S. Imports from Netherlands, 2005 (in $ millions)

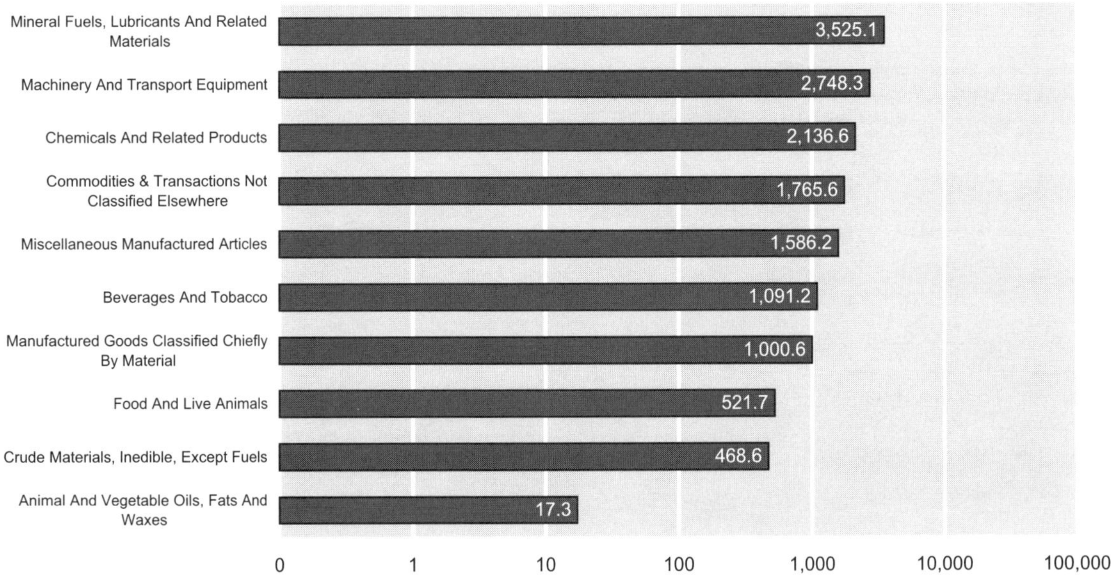

Source: Bureau of Economic Analysis, International Monetary Fund; Office of Trade and Industry Information

Norway & the United States
Investment and Trade Figures

Investment

The investment balance favors Norway, with U.S. investment totaling $8.8 billion in 2005 versus $6.1 billion of U.S. investment in Norway. U.S. assets in Norway were five times larger than Norway's assets in the United States. The employment balance favors Norway, with U.S. foreign affiliates employing close to 34,000 Norwegian workers in 2004.

Norway - U.S. Global Linkages, 2004
($ billions)

	U.S. in Norway	Norway in U.S.
Foreign Direct Investment* (2005)	8.8	6.1
Total Assets of Affiliates	37.7	6.5
Foreign Affiliate Sales	27.4	9.0
Value Added of Affiliates	14.3	0.9
Affiliate Employees	33,400	9,500

*Based on a historic-cost basis, data for 2005; gross product for majority-owned affiliates

Trade

Norwegian exports to the U.S. totaled over $6.9 billion in 2005, and were heavily skewed towards mineral fuels (i.e. petroleum products). The U.S. accounted for just 6.7% of total Norwegian exports, but nearly 34.5% when Norway's trade with the EU flows are excluded. Imports from the U.S. into Norway totaled $2.7 billion—that equates to 5% of total Norwegian imports or 16.2% excluding Norway's trade with the EU.

Top Ten U.S. Imports from Norway, 2005 (in $ millions)

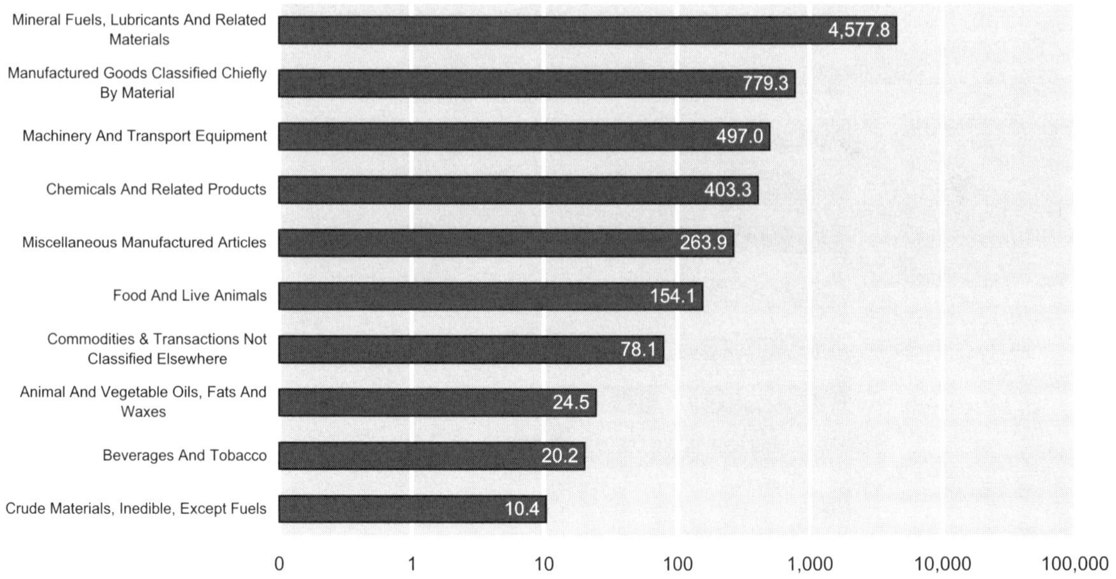

Source: Bureau of Economic Analysis, International Monetary Fund; Office of Trade and Industry Information

Poland & the United States

Investment and Trade Figures

Investment

As one of the largest markets in Central Europe, Poland has attracted significant sums of market-seeking U.S. foreign direct investment. At $16.8 billion, the U.S. asset base in Poland is larger than America's asset base in small developed nations like Finland or Greece. The U.S. affiliate work force of 90,700 workers is among the largest in all of Europe.

Poland - U.S. Global Linkages, 2004
($ billions)

	U.S. in Poland	Poland in U.S.
Foreign Direct Investment* (2005)	5.7	-
Total Assets of Affiliates	16.8	-
Foreign Affiliate Sales	16.7	-
Value Added of Affiliates	4.6	-
Affiliate Employees	90,700	-

*Based on a historic-cost basis, data for 2005; gross product for majority-owned affiliates

Trade

U.S. imports from Poland have increased sharply over the past few years, clearing $1.9 billion in 2005 from just $700 million in 1997. Imports run the gamut - from heavy machinery, to electronic goods, to iron and steel.

Top Ten U.S. Imports from Poland, 2005 (in $ millions)

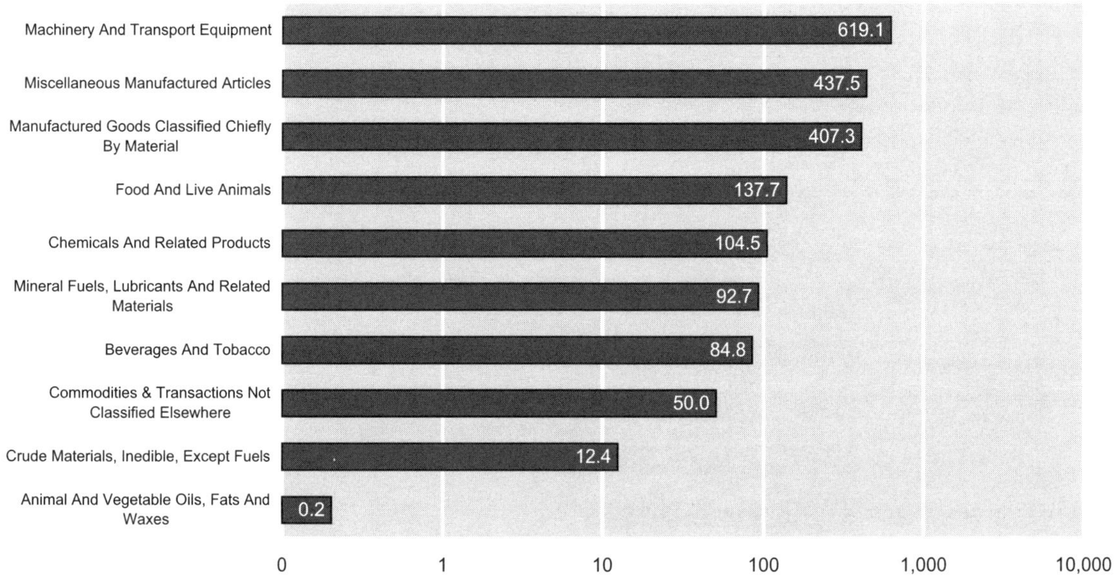

Source: Bureau of Economic Analysis, International Monetary Fund; Office of Trade and Industry Information

Portugal & the United States

Investment and Trade Figures

Investment

U.S. investment in Portugal totaled $2.7 billion in 2005, while U.S. affiliates employed some 31,300 Portuguese workers. Comparable data showing Portugal's investment in the U.S. is not available.

Portugal - U.S. Global Linkages, 2004 ($ billions)	U.S. in Portugal	Portugal in U.S.
Foreign Direct Investment* (2005)	2.7	-
Total Assets of Affiliates	27.6	-
Foreign Affiliate Sales	9.2	-
Value Added of Affiliates	5.2	-
Affiliate Employees	31,300	-

*Based on a historic-cost basis, data for 2005; gross product for majority-owned affiliates

Trade

Portuguese exports to the U.S. totaled $2.1 billion in 2005, while imports from the U.S. amounted to just $1.3 billion. The U.S. accounted for 5.4% of total exports but a hefty 23% share of Portugal's exports excluding intra-EU exports. Portuguese imports from the U.S. were 2.2% of total imports from the world in 2004 and 8.2% ex. intra-EU imports.

Top Ten U.S. Imports from Portugal, 2005 (in $ millions)

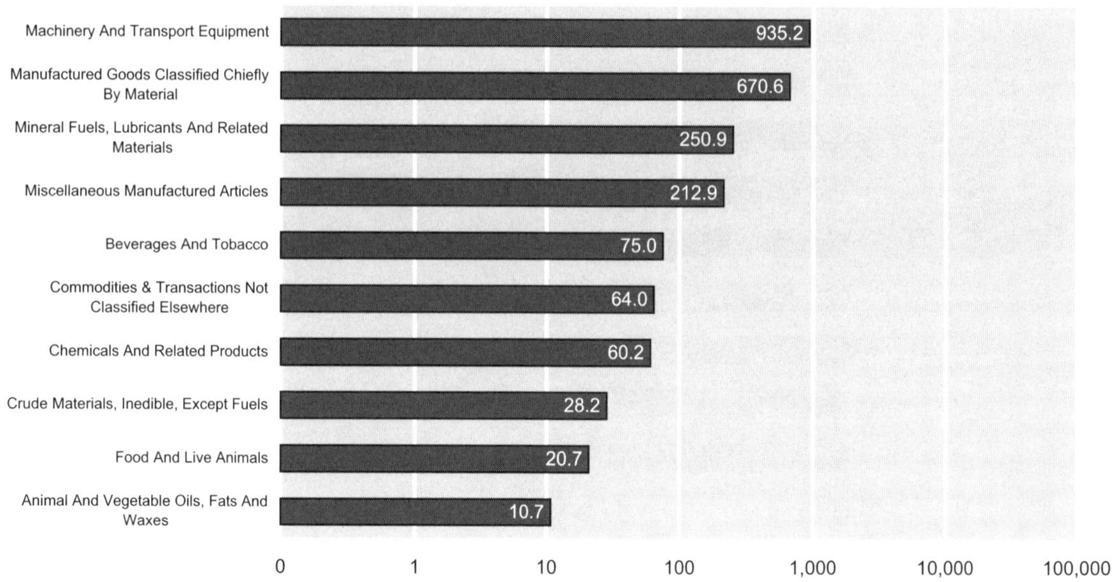

Source: Bureau of Economic Analysis, International Monetary Fund; Office of Trade and Industry Information

Romania & the United States

Investment and Trade Figures

Investment

America's asset base in Romania is rather small, with assets totaling just $1.5 billion in 2004. However, with Romania's inclusion into the EU, more U.S. firms are expected to increase their presence in Romania - albeit modestly - over the medium-term.

Romania - U.S. Global Linkages, 2004 ($ billions)	U.S. in Romania	Romania in U.S.
Foreign Direct Investment* (2005)	0.7	-
Total Assets of Affiliates	1.5	-
Foreign Affiliate Sales	2.0	-
Value Added of Affiliates	0.6	-
Affiliate Employees	18,600	-

*Based on a historic-cost basis, data for 2005; gross product for majority-owned affiliates

Trade

U.S. imports from Romania totaled $1.1 billion in 2005, a gradual rise from the levels of the late 1990s. Imports included a variety of manufactured goods. The U.S. is a rather small supplier to Romania, with the U.S. accounting for less than 3% of the nation's total imports.

Top Ten U.S. Imports from Romania, 2005 (in $ millions)

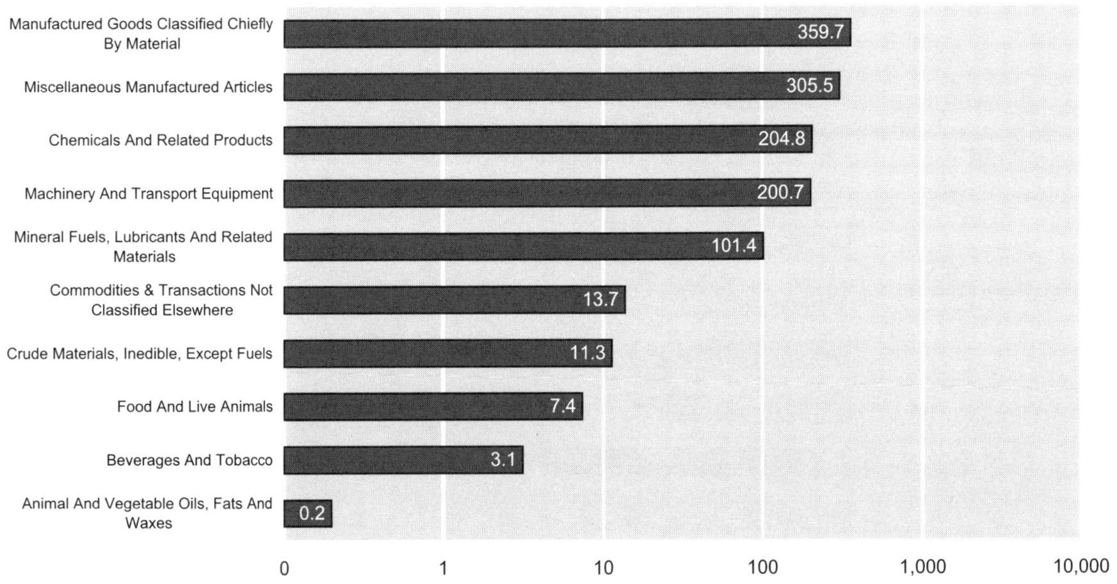

Source: Bureau of Economic Analysis, International Monetary Fund; Office of Trade and Industry Information

Slovakia & the United States

Investment and Trade Figures

Investment

America's asset base in Slovakia is small but expanding — total assets of U.S. affiliates in 2004 amounted to $3.9 billion, while foreign affiliate sales reached $5 billion. Centered in the heart of eastern Europe, the nation is well positioned to capture U.S. investment in distribution, transportation, wholesale trade and other service-like activities. U.S. affiliates employed 34,600 workers in 2004, among the largest work forces in eastern Europe.

Slovakia - U.S. Global Linkages, 2004 ($ billions)	U.S. in Slovakia	Slovakia in U.S.
Foreign Direct Investment* (2005)	0.1	-
Total Assets of Affiliates	3.9	-
Foreign Affiliate Sales	5.0	-
Value Added of Affiliates	1.5	-
Affiliate Employees	34,600	-

*Based on a historic-cost basis, data for 2005; gross product for majority-owned affiliates

Trade

U.S. imports from Slovakia have surged, rising to over $1.0 billion in 2005 from levels under $200 million in the late 1990s. Accounting for the surge has been rising motor vehicle imports from foreign affiliates producing in the country. Other imports include nuclear reactors, footwear and rubber.

Top Ten U.S. Imports from Slovakia, 2005 (in $ millions)

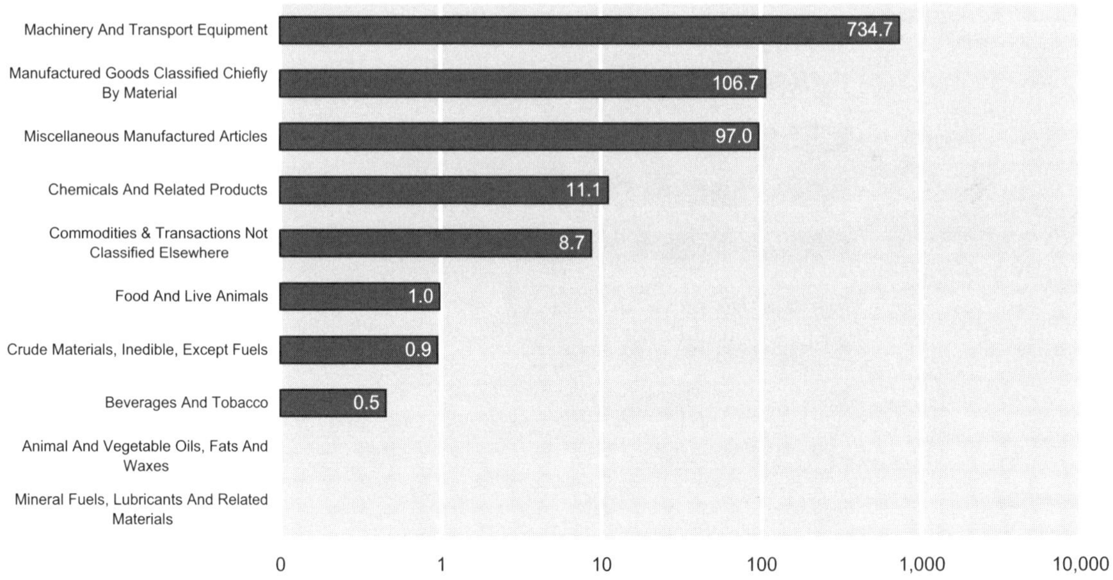

Source: Bureau of Economic Analysis, International Monetary Fund; Office of Trade and Industry Information

Slovenia & the United States
Investment and Trade Figures

Investment

Slovenia has experienced a gradual rise in U.S. foreign investment over the past few years. Total assets of affiliates amounted to $600 million in 2004. The country is expected to emerge as a bridge to the Balkan states over the next decade.

Slovenia - U.S. Global Linkages, 2004 ($ billions)	U.S. in Slovenia	Slovenia in U.S.
Foreign Direct Investment* (2005)	0.1	-
Total Assets of Affiliates	0.7	-
Foreign Affiliate Sales	0.7	-
Value Added of Affiliates	0.3	-
Affiliate Employees	4,300	-

*Based on a historic-cost basis, data for 2005; gross product for majority-owned affiliates

Trade

U.S. imports from Slovenia totaled $400 million in 2005, a gradual rise from the levels of the late 1990s. Imports included chemicals, furniture and glassware.

Top Ten U.S. Imports from Slovenia, 2005 (in $ millions)

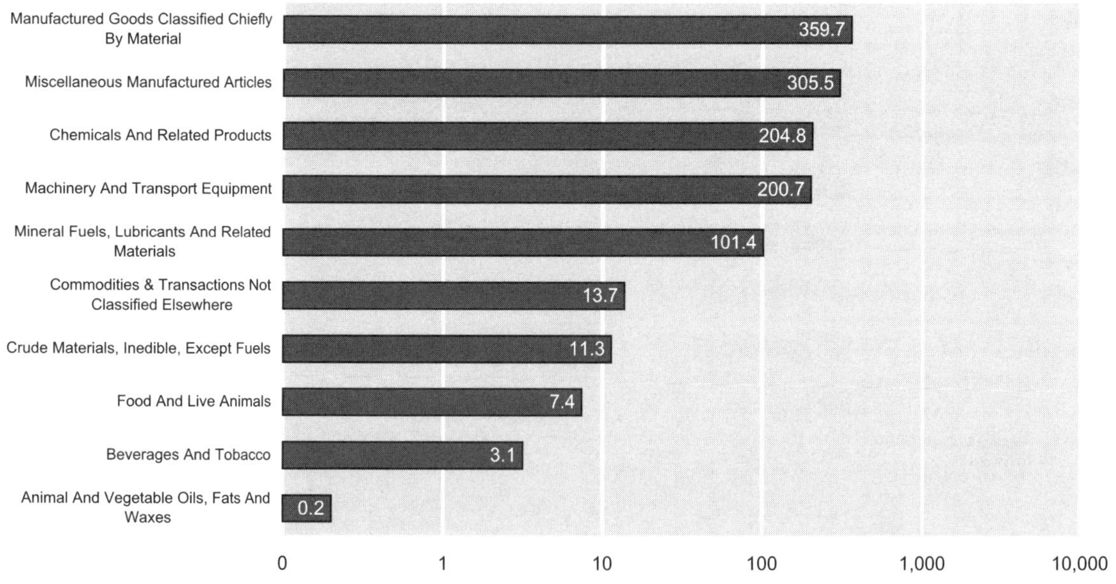

Source: Bureau of Economic Analysis, International Monetary Fund; Office of Trade and Industry Information

Spain & the United States
Investment and Trade Figures

Investment

The investment balance favors Spain in 2005, with U.S. investment in Spain ($43.3 billion) more than six times the size of total Spanish investment in the U.S. ($7.1 billion). The U.S. is not a strategic priority to Spanish firms, with Spanish affiliates' assets in the U.S. totaling just $7.4 billion in 2004, while affiliate sales in the U.S. totaled just $6.7 billion. The employment balance is heavily skewed in favor of Spain.

Spain - U.S. Global Linkages, 2004
($ billions)

	U.S. in Spain	Spain in U.S.
Foreign Direct Investment* (2005)	43.3	7.1
Total Assets of Affiliates	112.4	7.4
Foreign Affiliate Sales	68.8	6.7
Value Added of Affiliates	14.8	1.3
Affiliate Employees	197,200	20,200

*Based on a historic-cost basis, data for 2005; gross product for majority-owned affiliates

Trade

The U.S. received just 4% of total exports from Spain in 2005, but a share of 13.7% of total exports when intra-EU trade is excluded. Regarding imports, the U.S. supplied 2.9% of total imports by Spain in 2005, although the share rises to 7.7% after accounting for intra-EU trade.

Top Ten U.S. Imports from Spain, 2005 (in $ millions)

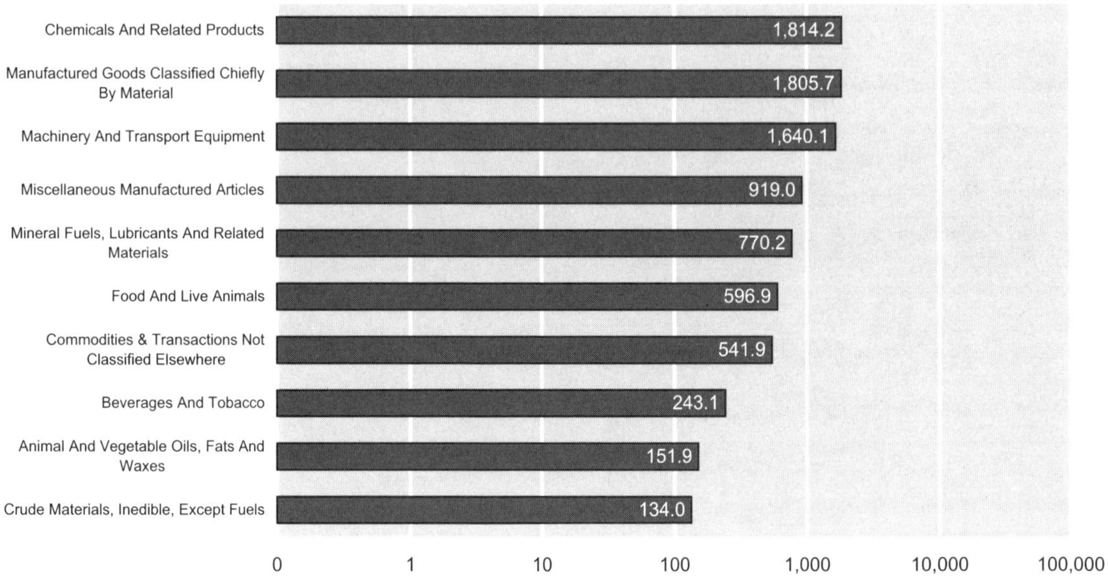

Source: Bureau of Economic Analysis, International Monetary Fund; Office of Trade and Industry Information

Sweden & the United States

Investment and Trade Figures

Investment

The investment balance favors Sweden, with American investment in the Nordic country totaling $33.4 billion, approximately 34.8% larger than the $24.8 billion Swedish firms invested in the U.S. in 2005. The asset base of U.S. affiliates in Sweden was nearly three times larger than the $36.3 billion Swedish affiliates held in the U.S.; the employment balance is heavily in favor of the United States.

Sweden - U.S. Global Linkages, 2004 ($ billions)	U.S. in Sweden	Sweden in U.S.
Foreign Direct Investment* (2005)	33.4	24.8
Total Assets of Affiliates	107.1	36.3
Foreign Affiliate Sales	54.0	44.0
Value Added of Affiliates	11.0	12.5
Affiliate Employees	101,200	207,800

*Based on a historic-cost basis, data for 2005; gross product for majority-owned affiliates

Trade

The U.S. is a fairly large export market for Sweden, with exports to the U.S. ($13.8 billlon in 2005) accounting for 10.6% of the global total and nearly 24.4% of the total ex. intra-EU trade. Swedish imports of $4.0 billion from the U.S. accounted for 3.6% of Sweden's total imports in 2005, although the share rises to 11.1% ex. intra-EU imports.

Top Ten U.S. Imports from Sweden, 2005 (in $ millions)

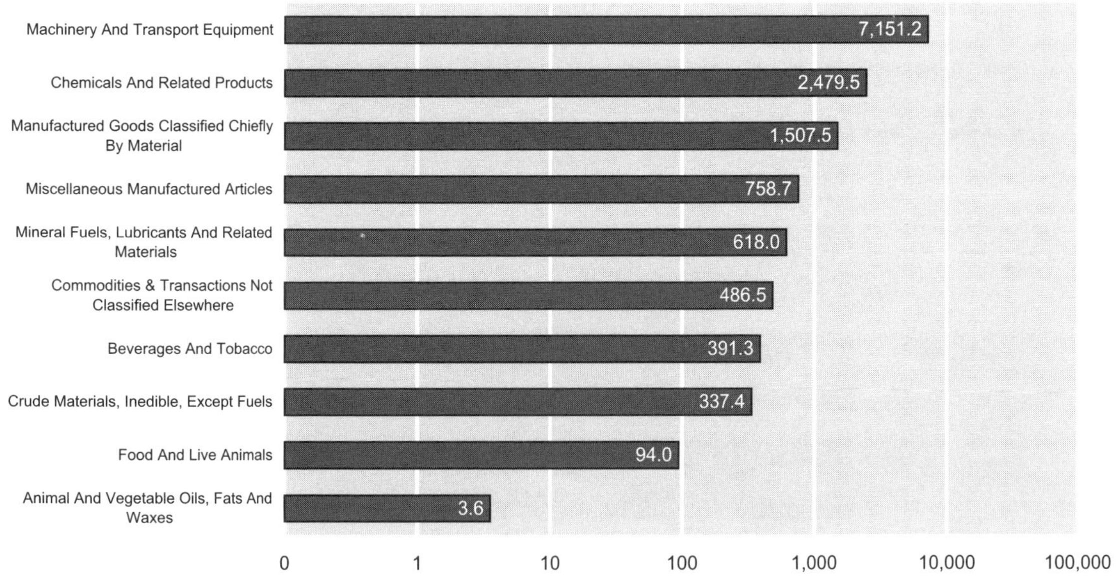

Source: Bureau of Economic Analysis, International Monetary Fund; Office of Trade and Industry Information

Switzerland & the United States

Investment and Trade Figures

Investment

The investment balance favors the U.S.— investment in Switzerland totaled $83.4 billion in 2005 versus $122.4 billion of Swiss investment in the U.S. Switzerland has one of the largest asset bases in the U.S. of any nation at $1.134 trillion (mainly in services like insurance and financial services) and was roughly four times that of U.S. affiliates in Switzerland. The employment balance significantly favors the United States.

Switzerland - U.S. Global Linkages, 2004
($ billions)

	U.S. in Switzerland	Switzerland in U.S.
Foreign Direct Investment* (2005)	83.4	122.4
Total Assets of Affiliates	293.9	1,134.5
Foreign Affiliate Sales	135.2	129.7
Value Added of Affiliates	17.6	32.4
Affiliate Employees	67,300	383,200

*Based on a historic-cost basis, data for 2005; gross product for majority-owned affiliates

Trade

Swiss exports to the U.S. totaled $14.3 billion in 2005, representing 10.9% of all Swiss exports, and 29% when taken as a share of exports to regions outside the EU. In the same year, Switzerland imported American goods worth $7.1 billion, approximately 5.6% of the global total, yet when imports from the EU were excluded, U.S. goods comprised over 28% of Swiss imports.

Top Ten U.S. Imports from Switzerland, 2005 (in $ millions)

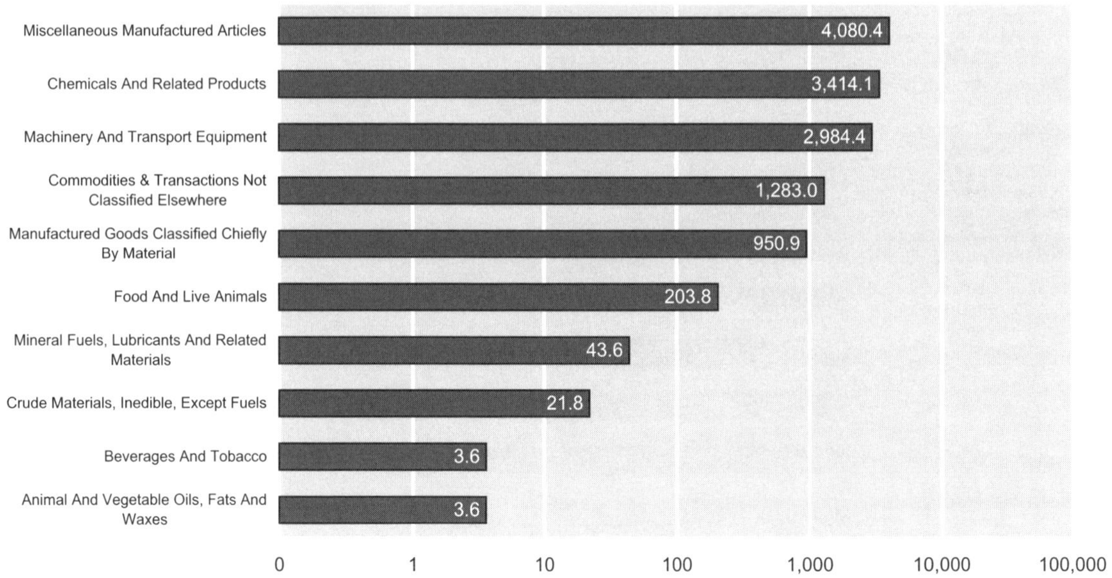

Source: Bureau of Economic Analysis, International Monetary Fund; Office of Trade and Industry Information

United Kingdom & the United States

Investment and Trade Figures

Investment

The U.S.-U.K. investment balance is fairly even, however the U.S. had a larger presence in the U.K in 2005. Value added by American and British affiliates totaled $132.5 billion and $107.2 billion, respectively. U.S. foreign affiliate sales in the United Kingdom totaled $436.2 billion, the largest country total in the world. And, although down from peak levels reached at the beginning of the decade, British affiliates employed over 1 million Americans in 2004, while American affiliates employed over 900,000 workers in the UK.

United Kingdom - U.S. Global Linkages, 2004 ($ billions)	U.S. in United Kingdom	United Kingdom in U.S.
Foreign Direct Investment* (2005)	323.8	282.5
Total Assets of Affiliates	1,884.3	1,018.3
Foreign Affiliate Sales	436.2	372.2
Value Added of Affiliates	132.5	107.2
Affiliate Employees	1,166,300	920,800

*Based on a historic-cost basis, data for 2005; gross product for majority-owned affiliates

Trade

Bilateral trade flows are strong between the United Kingdom and the United States. Exports to the U.S. totaled $56 billion in 2005, some 15% of total exports from United Kingdom and 32.5% when intra-EU exports are excluded from the global sum. Top exports to the U.S. include heavy machinery and chemical products. The U.S. was a key supplier to the United Kingdom in 2005, with $41.9 billion in imports from the U.S accounting for 8.7% of imports from the world and 17.5% ex. intra-EU trade.

Top Ten U.S. Imports from United Kingdom, 2005 (in $ millions)

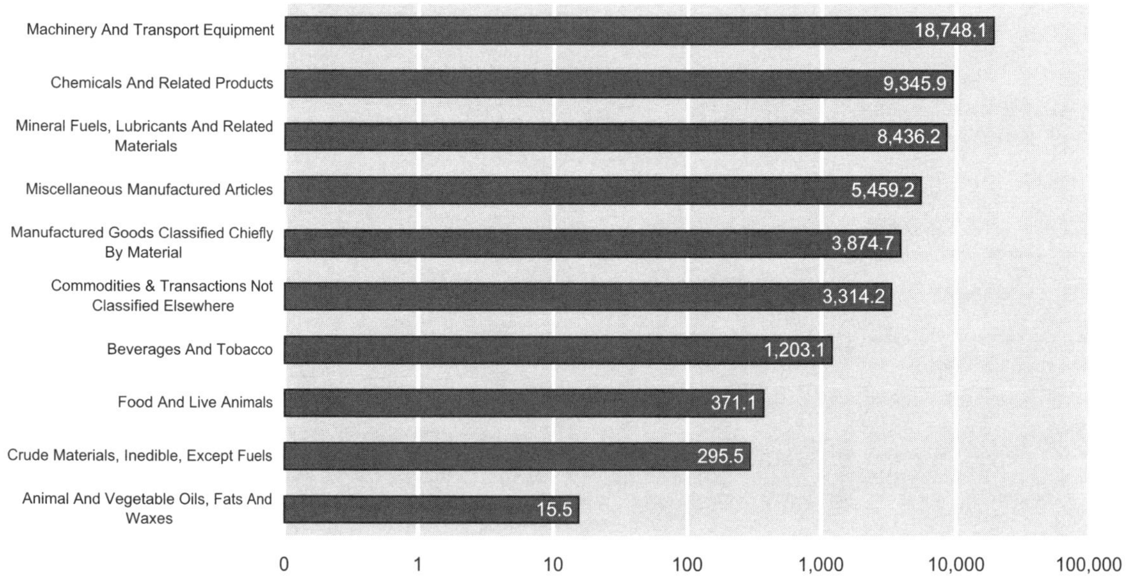

Source: Bureau of Economic Analysis, International Monetary Fund; Office of Trade and Industry Information

Notes on Data and Sources

Employment, Investment, and Trade Linkages for the 50 U.S. States and Europe

Data for investment as well as investment related jobs are from the U.S. Commerce Department's Bureau of Economic Analysis. Investment data measure gross property, plant, and equipment of affiliates. Europe includes Belgium, France, Germany, Italy, Netherlands, Sweden, Switzerland, and the United Kingdom. Trade data are from the International Trade Administration's Office of Trade and Industry Information at the U.S. Commerce Department. Europe includes Andorra, Austria, Belgium, Bosnia-Herzegovina, Bulgaria, Croatia, Cyprus, Denmark, Faeroe Islands, Finland, France, Germany, Gibraltar, Greece, Iceland, Ireland, Italy, Liechtenstein, Luxembourg, Macedonia, Malta and Gozo, Monaco, Netherlands, Norway, Portugal, Romania, San Marino, Slovenia, Spain, Sweden, Switzerland, Turkey, United Kingdom, Vatican City, Yugoslavia. The top ten exports to Europe bar chart employs a logarithmic scale to facilitate cross state comparisons.

Investment and Trade for the EU 27, Norway and Switzerland and the U.S.

Investment data are from the Bureau of Economic Analysis. Trade data are from the IMF Trade Statistics. Data for the top ten U.S. imports bar charts are from the Office of Trade and Industry Information of the International Trade Administration. They employ logarithmic scales to facilitate cross-country comparisons.

About the Authors

Daniel S. Hamilton and **Joseph P. Quinlan** have authored and edited a series of award-winning books and articles on the modern transatlantic economy, including *Protecting Our Prosperity: Ensuring Both National Security and the Benefits of Foreign Investment in the United States* (2006); *The Transatlantic Economy 2005* (2006); *Deep Integration: How Transatlantic Markets are Leading Globalization* (2005); and *Partners in Prosperity: The Changing Geography of the Transatlantic Economy* (2004). Together they were recipients of the 2006 Transatlantic Business Award by the American Chamber of Commerce to the European Union.

Daniel S. Hamilton is the Richard von Weizsäcker Professor and Director of the Center for Transatlantic Relations at the Paul H. Nitze School of Advanced International Studies, Johns Hopkins University. He also serves as Executive Director of the American Consortium on EU Studies (ACES), designated by the European Commission as the EU Center of Excellence Washington, DC. He is principal advisor to the Congressional Caucus on the EU, and has served as Deputy Assistant Secretary of State.

Joseph P. Quinlan is a Fellow at the Center for Transatlantic Relations, with extensive experience in the U.S. corporate sector. He is a leading expert on the transatlantic economy and well-known global economist/strategist on Wall Street. He specializes in global capital flows, international trade and multinational strategies. He lectures at New York University, and his publications have appeared in such venues as *Foreign Affairs*, the *Financial Times* and the *Wall Street Journal*.